||| ||| || | || | ||||| | | ||||||| | || |||||
W9-CFC-568

mustsees
WASHINGTON, DC

Washington Monument and the Capitol   Photo: Destination DC

Editorial Director   Cynthia Clayton Ochterbeck

mustsees Washington, DC

Editor   Rachel Mills
Principal Writer   Beth Kanter
Production Manager   Natasha G. George
Cartography   Peter Wrenn
Photo Editor   Yoshimi Kanazawa
Proofreaders   Jonathan P. Gilbert, Alison Coupe
Layout   Chris Bell, Natasha G. George
Cover & Interior Design   Chris Bell

Contact Us: Michelin Maps and Guides
                                  One Parkway South
                                  Greenville, SC 29615
                                  USA
                                  www.michelintravel.com
                                  michelin.guides@us.michelin.com

                                  Michelin Maps and Guides
                                  Hannay House
                                  39 Clarendon Road
                                  Watford, Herts WD17 1JA
                                  UK
                                  ☎(01923) 205 240
                                  www.ViaMichelin.com
                                  travelpubsales@uk.michelin.com

Special Sales: For information regarding bulk sales, customized
                                  editions and premium sales, please contact
                                  our Customer Service Departments:
                                  USA   1-800-432-6277
                                  UK   (01923) 205 240
                                  Canada   1-800-361-8236

Michelin Apa Publications Ltd
A joint venture between Michelin and Langenscheidt
58 Borough High Street, London SE1 1XF, United Kingdom

No part of this publication may be reproduced in any form
without the prior permission of the publisher.

© 2009 Michelin Apa Publications Ltd
ISBN 978-1-906261-65-8
Printed: December 2008
Printed and bound: Himmer, Germany

Note to the reader:
While every effort is made to ensure that all information printed in this guide is correct and
up-to-date, Michelin Apa Publications Ltd. accepts no liability for any direct, indirect or
consequential losses howsoever caused so far as such can be excluded by law. Admission
prices listed for sights in this guide are for a single adult, unless otherwise specified.

Welcome to Washington, DC

Destination DC

Smithsonian Castle

Introduction

Must See

p 67

p 113

p88

TABLE OF CONTENTS

★★★ATTRACTIONS

Unmissable attractions awarded three stars in this guide include:

Great Smoky Mountains
National Park   p 126

National Park Service

National World War II
Memorial   p 60

Destination DC

National Air and Space
Museum   p 30

Eric Long, National Air and Space
Museum, Smithsonian Institution

The Capitol   p 22

Jake McGuire/Destination DC

MUST KNOW

©The Colonial Williamsburg Foundation
Colonial Williamsburg p 118

©kuosumo/Fotolia.com
Washington Monument p 62

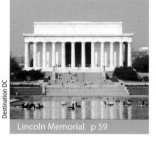
Destination DC
Lincoln Memorial p 59

Brigitta L. House/Michelin
White House p 23

©PhotoDisc
Mount Vernon p 106

★★★ ATTRACTIONS

Unmissable sights in and around Washington

For more than 75 years people have used the Michelin stars to take the guesswork out of travel. Our star-rating system helps you make the best decision on where to go, what to do, and what to see.

★★★	Absolutely Must See
★★	Really Must See
★	Must See
No Star	See

MUST KNOW

 ACTIVITIES

**Unmissable Washington tours,
shopping and more**
We recommend every activity in
this guide, but the Michelin Man
highlights our top picks.

Bars & Clubs
Black Cat *p 100*
Eighteenth Street Lounge *p 101*
Nightclub 9:30 *p 103*

Hotels
The Hotel George *p 146*
Hotel Monaco *p 150*

Kids
Pandas at the National Zoo *p 89*
Imagination Stage *p 91*
Puppet Co. Playhouse at
    Glenn Echo *p 92*

Recreation
Nationals Park
    Baseball Stadium *p 19*
The National Gallery of Art
    Sculpture Garden Ice Skating *p 84*
Paddleboating
    on the Tidal Basin *p 92*

Restaurants
Mitisam Native Foods Cafe:
    National Museum of the
    American Indian *p 45*
Brunch at Georgia Brown's *p 134*
Ben's Chili Bowl *p 140*

Shopping
Penn Quarter Freshfarm
    Market *p 79*
Kramerbooks *p 97*
Politics and Prose bookstore *p 97*
Apartment Zero *p 99*
Barston's Child's Play *p 99*
Periwinkle *p 99*
Zenith Gallery *p 99*

Take a Break
Ching Ching CHA House of
    Tea *p 96*
Cakelove and Love Cafe *p 98*
Firehook Bakery and
    Coffee House *p 99*
Afternoon tea at the Renaissance
    Mayflower hotel *p 147*

Theatres and Arts
AMC Loews Uptown 1 *p 79*
Screen on the Green *p 84*
Musical Political Satire
    "Capitol Steps" *p 95*
Wolf Trap National Park for
    the Performing Arts *p 95*

Tours
The Monuments by Night *p 56*
On Location Tour *p 84*
Scandal Tour *p 86*

**Remember to Look-out for the
Michelin Man** *for the top activities.*

STAR ATTRACTIONS

CALENDAR OF EVENTS

Listed below is a selection of Washington, DC's most popular annual events. Note that dates may change from year to year. For more detailed information, contact Destination DC, the city's convention and visitors bureau *(202-789-7000; www.washington.org).*

January

Dr. Martin Luther King Birthday Observance
202-619-7222
The Mall
www.nps.gov and
www.mlkday.gov

February

Abraham Lincoln's Birthday
202-619-7222
Lincoln Memorial
www.nps.gov
Black History Month
202-357-2700
Various locations
www.washington.org
Chinese New Year Parade
202-271-7002
Chinatown
www.chinatownchamber.us

March

National Cherry Blossom Festival
661-7584
Tidal Basin
www.nationalcherryblossom
festival.org
Washington Home and Garden Show
703-823-7960
Washington Convention Center
www.washingtonhomeand
gardenshow.com

April

Easter Egg Roll
202-456-7041
White House Grounds
www.whitehouse.gov

Easter Sunrise Service
703-607-8000
Arlington National Cemetery
www.arlingtoncemetery.org
Filmfest DC
202-628-3456
Various locations
www.filmfestdc.org
Shakespeare's Birthday
202-544-4600
Folger Shakespeare Library
www.folger.edu

May

National Memorial Day Concert
202-619-7222
Capitol (west lawn)
www.pbs.org/memorialday
concert

Cherry blossoms by the Jefferson Memorial

Destination DC

June

Dance Africa DC
202-269-1600
Dance Place, 3225 8th St. NE
www.danceplace.org
Dupont-Kalorama Museum Walk
202-667-0441
Dupont Circle
www.dkmuseums.com

Smithsonian Folklife Festival

Jeff Tinsley/Smithsonian Institution

July
National Independence Day Celebration
202-619-7222
The Mall
www.nps.gov
Smithsonian Folklife Festival
202-633-6440
The Mall
www.folklife.si.edu

August
Legg Mason Tennis Classic
202-721-9500
William H.G. Fitzgerald Tennis Center
www.leggmasontennis classic.com

September
Adams Morgan Day
202-232-1960
Columbia Rd. & 18th St.
www.ammainstreet.org
International Children's Festival
703-642-0862
Wolf Trap Farm Park, Vienna, VA
www.artsfairfax.org
National Symphony Labor Day Concert
202-619-7222
Capitol (west lawn)
www.nps.gov

National Book Festival
888-714-4696
The Mall
www.loc.gov/bookfest

October
Columbus Day Observance
202-619-7222
Columbus Memorial Plaza
www.nps.gov
Fall Garden & Grounds Tour
202-208-1631
White House Grounds
www.whitehouse.gov
Marine Corps Marathon
703-784-2225
Marine Corps War Memorial
800-786-8762
www.marinemarathon.com

November
Veterans Day Ceremonies:
Arlington National Cemetery
703-607-8000
Vietnam Veterans Memorial
202-619-7222
US Navy Memorial
202-737-2300

December
Christmas Celebration
202-537-6200
Washington National Cathedral
www.cathedral.org
Lighting of National Christmas Tree & Pageant of Peace
202-208-1631
The Ellipse
www.nps.gov/whho/pageant
White House Candelight Christmas Tour
202-456-7041
White House
www.whitehouse.gov

PRACTICAL INFORMATION

WHEN TO GO

The short answer to "when to go?" is—now. A pilgrimage to the nation's capital is a must for history buffs and patriots as well as lovers of beautiful, energetic cities. That said, spring is Washington's peak tourist season, when mild temperatures and the blossoming of the famous cherry trees *(late Mar–early Apr)* attract crowds of visitors. Make hotel reservations well in advance and expect long lines at the major sights during the spring and the hot, humid summer, when long days, extended operating hours for many sights, and numerous outdoor events draw tourists. In the fall, temperatures are moderate, crowds thin out and the autumn foliage is spectacular. Winter months can bring snow, but severe snowstorms are infrequent.

KNOW BEFORE YOU GO

Before you go, contact the following tourist organizations in the DC Metropolitan Area.

Visitor Centers

Destination DC
901 7th St. NW, 4th Floor,
Washington, DC 20001
202-789-7000
www.washington.org

Washington, DC Visitors Information Center
Ronald Reagan International Trade Center Building
1300 Pennsylvania Ave. NW,
Washington, DC 20004
202-289-8317 or 866-324-7386
www.dcchamber.org

Alexandria Convention and Visitors Association
221 King Street
Alexandria, VA 22314
703-838-4200 or 800-388-9119
www.visitalexandriava.com

Arlington Visitors Center
1301 South Joyce St., Suite D11
Arlington, VA 22202
703-416-0784 or 800-677-6267
www.stayarlington.com

International Visitors

Visitors from outside the US can obtain information from Destination DC *(202-789-7000; www.washington.org)* or from the US embassy or consulate in their country of residence. For a complete list of American consulates and embassies abroad, visit the US State Department Bureau of Consular Affairs listing on the Internet at: *http://travel.state.gov.*

Seasonal Temperatures in Washington, DC (recorded at National Airport)				
	Jan	**Apr**	**July**	**Oct**
Average High	43°F / 6°C	67°F / 19°C	88°F / 31°C	69°F / 21°C
Average Low	28°F / -2°C	46°F / 8°C	70°F / 20°C	50°F / 10°C

In The News

The city's leading daily paper, the *Washington Post (www.washingtonpost.com)* lists entertainment, special events, and attractions for children in the Friday Weekend section; the Sunday edition contains a section highlighting the performing arts. The Post also publishes the day's congressional and Supreme Court schedules.

Entry Requirements

Since October 1, 2003, travelers entering the United States under the Visa Waiver Program (VWP) must have a machine-readable passport. Any traveler without a machine-readable passport will be required to obtain a visa before entering the US. Citizens of VWP countries are permitted to enter the US for general business or tourist purposes for a maximum of 90 days without needing a visa. Requirements for the Visa Waiver Program can be found at the Department of State's Visa Services website *(http://travel.state.gov/visa/visa_1750.html)*.

All citizens of nonparticipating countries must have a visitor's visa. Upon entry, nonresident foreign visitors must present a valid passport and round-trip transportation ticket. Canadian citizens are also now required to have documents to establish citizenship, a valid passport is recommended.

US Customs

All articles brought into the US must be declared at the time of entry. Prohibited items: plant material; firearms and ammunition (if not for sporting purposes); meat or poultry products. For information, contact the US Customs Service, 1300 Pennsylvania Ave. NW, Washington, DC 20229 *(877-227-5511; www.customs.gov)*.

Driving in the US

Visitors bearing valid driver's licenses issued by their country of residence are not required to obtain an International Driver's License. Drivers must carry vehicle registration and/or rental contract, and proof of automobile insurance at all times. Always drive on the right-hand side of the road.

GETTING THERE

By Air

The Washington, DC area is served by three airports, two in Virginia and one in Maryland:

Ronald Reagan Washington National Airport (DCA) – 4.5mi south of downtown DC, in Alexandria, Virginia *(703-417-8000; www.mwaa.com)*.

Dulles International Airport (IAD) – 26mi west of downtown DC, in Loudoun County, Virginia *(703-572-2700; www.mwaa.com)*.

Baltimore-Washington International Thurgood Marshall Airport (BWI) – Off I-195, 28mi north of downtown DC and 8mi south of Baltimore, MD *(800-435-9294; www.bwiairport.com)*.

By Train

Union Station is Washington's only railroad station and offers Amtrak and other rail service. Located near Capitol Hill at Massachusetts and Delaware Aves. NE, the station is accessible by Metrorail (Red Line). Maryland Rail Commuter Service

PRACTICAL INFORMATION

Congressional Visits

Tickets for congressional visits and special tours of some of DC's more popular sites *(listed below)* may be obtained by writing to your senators or representative. As each member of Congress is allotted a limited number of tickets, requests should be made several months in advance. These visits, which are generally scheduled early in the morning, are more extensive than the standard tours and, best of all, you avoid the long lines.

Members of Congress can arrange special tours for the following sites:

- Bureau of Engraving and Printing
- Capitol Building Gallery
- Supreme Court
- Treasury Department
- White House
- National Cathedral
- State Department
- Kennedy Center
- Library of Congress
- National Archives

When writing your Congress member to request tours, be sure to include:

Your name, address & daytime phone number
Sites you would like to tour
Number of individuals in your group
Dates you will be visiting DC

Visiting Your Senators or Representatives – If you would like to meet the elected officials who represent you in Congress, you should write two to three months in advance to request an appointment. Call the Capitol *(202-225-6827)* or write:

US Senate
Washington, DC 20510

US House
Washington, DC 20515

(MARC) operates trains between DC and Baltimore on weekdays. *For schedules and routes, call 800-872-7245 or visit www.amtrak.com.*

By Bus
The capital's main bus terminal is at 1005 1st Street NE, a short walk from Union Station. *For fares, schedules and routes, call 800-231-2222 or visit www.greyhound.com.*

By Car
Washington is situated at the crossroads of several major interstate routes: I-95 (north–south), I-66 (east), Route 50 (west) and I-270 (northwest). These and other roads leading to the capital connect with the Capital Beltway

(I-495), which encircles the city about 12mi from the center.

GETTING AROUND

The Quadrant System
Based on L'Enfant's design, the layout of DC's streets is logical. The focal point of Washington's street system is the US Capitol building. From this prominent landmark, the two cardinal axes—North Capitol and South Capitol streets, and East Capitol Street and the Mall—divide the city into four quadrants: Northwest, Northeast, Southeast and Southwest.

Numbered streets running north–south are laid out in ascending order on either side of North and

Car Rental Companies

Company	Reservations	Internet
Alamo	800-327-9633	www.alamo.com
Avis	800-831-2847	www.avis.com
Budget	800-527-0700	www.drivebudget.com
Dollar	800-800-4000	www.dollar.com
Enterprise	800-736-8222	www.enterprise.com
Hertz	800-654-3131	www.hertz.com
National	800-227-7368	www.nationalcar.com
Thrifty	800-331-4200	www.thrifty.com

South Capitol Streets, while lettered streets running east–west begin on either side of the Mall/East Capitol axis. This arrangement gives rise to two sets of numbered streets and two sets of lettered streets. Since the same address may be found in each of the four quadrants, it is imperative that the appropriate designation (NE, SE, SW, NW) be attached to the address to avoid confusion. Avenues bearing the names of the states of the Union run diagonally across the grid pattern and generally radiate from circles named after prominent Americans such as Washington, Sheridan and Dupont.

Note the following exceptions:
In the NW and SW quadrants there is no A Street owing to the location of the Mall; B Street is replaced by Constitution Avenue (NE and NW) and Independence Avenue (SE and SW); there is no J Street. Lettered streets end at W, beyond which a new alphabetical series begins with two-syllable names (Adams, Bryant, etc.). *For information about how to find an address in DC, see back cover flap.*

By Car
The use of seat belts is mandatory for driver and passengers. Child safety seats are required for children under eight years (seats are available from rental-car agencies). Drivers must always yield the right of way to pedestrians. In the city, street parking is limited and parking regulations are strictly enforced. Arterial streets in the District have posted rush-hour restrictions that prohibit parking from 7am–9:30am and 4pm–6:30pm. Parking signs are color-coded: green-and-white signs indicate hours when parking is allowed; red-and-white signs indicate hours when parking is not allowed. Parking spaces for permit holders only (diplomatic or government vehicles) are reserved 24 hours daily unless otherwise specified.

Public Transport
The Washington Metropolitan Area Transit Authority (*202-637-7000; www.wmata.com*) operates a public rapid-transit (Metrorail) and bus (Metrobus) system that links Washington, DC and areas of Maryland and Northern Virginia.

15

Emergency (Police/Ambulance/Fire Department, 24hrs)	911
Police (non-emergency)	311
Hotel Docs (24hrs)	800-468-3537
Dental Referral (Mon-Fri 8am-4pm)	202-547-7615
24-hour Pharmacies:	
CVS, 6 Dupont Circle NW	202-785-1466
CVS, 1199 Vermont Ave. NW (Thomas Circle)	202-628-0720
Poison Control Center (24hrs)	202-625-3333
Time	202-844-2525
Weather	202-936-1212

Subway

The Metrorail subway system, known locally as the Metro, carries commuters to and from the suburbs during peak commuting hours and is a convenient, safe and inexpensive way to get around while sightseeing in the city. *For map and details about the subway, see inside back cover.*

City Buses

Metrobuses operate daily *(hours differ by route, for information, call 202-637-7000 or visit www.wmata. com)*. Bus stops are indicated by red, white and blue signs. Buses display the route number and final destination above the windshield. Fares are determined by the time of day and length of trip *(base fare is $1.35; exact fare required)*; fares are higher during peak commuting hours.

Taxis

Numerous taxi companies operate under the DC Taxicab Commission *(202-645-6018; www.dctaxi.dc.gov)*. On June 1, 2008, all Washington DC taxis began using fare meters.

The base fare is $3.00 for the first 1/6 mile, with each additional 1/6 mile costing 25 cents. There is a $2.00 fee for each piece of large luggage stored in the trunk and an additional 50-cent charge for large luggage handled by the driver. $1.50 is added to the total fare for each additional passenger over the age of six and fuel and airport surcharges sometimes apply. The maximum fare within the District before surcharges is $19.00. Ride sharing in the District is only allowed from Union Station.

ACCESSIBILITY

Disabled Travelers

Federal law requires that businesses (including hotels and restaurants) provide access for the disabled, devices for the hearing impaired, and designated parking spaces. For information for disabled travelers, contact the Society for Accessible Travel and Hospitality (SATH), 347 Fifth Ave., Suite 605, New York, NY 10016 *(212-447-7284; www.sath.org)*. The Washington, D.C. Access Guide offers specific information for disabled travelers to the DC area *($5; Access Information, Inc., 21618 Slidell Rd., Boyds, MD 20841; 301-528-8664; www.disabilityguide.org)*. All national parks have facilities for the disabled and offer free or discounted passes *(contact the National Park Service, Office of Public Inquiries, P.O. Box 37127, Room 1013, Washington, DC 20013-7127; 202-208-4747; www.nps.gov)*. Passengers who will need assistance with train or bus travel should give advance notice to Amtrak *(800-872-7245 or 800-523-6590/TDD; www.amtrak.com)* or Greyhound *(800-231-2222 or 800-345-3109/TDD; www.greyhound.com)*. Reservations for hand-controlled rental cars should be made in advance.

ACCOMMODATIONS

For a list of suggested accommodations, see Must Stay.

Reservations Services
Accommodations Express; 800-277-1064; www.accommodationsexpress.com.
Capitol Reservations; 800-847-4832; www.washingtondchotels.com.
Washington DC Accommodations; 800-503-3330; www.wdcahotels.com.
Bed & Breakfast Accommodations Ltd.; 413-582-9888 or 877-893-3233; www.bnbaccom.com.

Alexandria & Arlington Bed and Breakfast Network; 703-549-3415 or 888-549-3415; www.aabbn.com.

Hostels – An economical option, the Washington International Youth Hostel *(1009 11th St. NW; 202-737-2333; www.hiwashington dc.org)* charges between $29 and $32/night (250 beds).

Campgrounds – Capitol KOA Campground *(410-923-2771 or 800-562-0248; www.koakamp grounds.com)*.

COMMUNICATIONS

Local calls made from payphones typically cost 50 cents. Calls between the District and the close-in suburbs of Maryland and Northern Virginia are considered local. An unofficial listing of DC payphones can be found online at www.pay phone-directory.org/paydc.html. Many coffee shops, restaurants, and hotels throughout the city offer Wireless Internet access. Free public wireless Internet access is also available in Dupont Circle and at several outdoor locations on the National Mall including the Enid A. Haupt Garden, the plaza in front of the Supreme Court, and the front steps of the Library of Congress. The Smithsonian Information Center is also a free "hotspot." The website http://ilovefreewifi.com lists free Wi-Fi spots.

Measurement Equivalents									
Degrees Fahrenheit 95°	86°	77°	68°	59°	50°	41°	32°	23°	14°
Degrees Celsius 35°	30°	25°	20°	15°	10°	5°	0°	-5°	-10°

1 inch = 2.54 centimeters
1 mile = 1.6 kilometers
1 quart = 0.9 liters

1 foot = 30.5 centimeters
1 pound = 0.45 kilograms
1 gallon = 3.8 liters

PRACTICAL INFORMATION

Area Codes
In DC you need to use the area code if you're dialing between two different area codes, but not within the 202 area code. In Virginia and Maryland, you need to always dial the area code first for any calls.

Washington, DC: 202
Suburban Maryland: 301, 240
Suburban Virginia: 703, 571
Eastern Maryland: 410, 443

DISCOUNTS
Many hotels, attractions and restaurants offer discounts to visitors age 62 or older (proof of age may be required). The **AARP** (formerly the American Association of Retired Persons; 601 E St. NW, Washington, DC 20049; 202-424-3410; www.aarp.com) offers discounts to its members. Senior citizens ride for half the regular fare on Metrorail and for 60¢ on most Metrobus routes (senior tickets sold at Metro sales office; see www.wmata.com for locations.

Most theaters in town also offer discounted same-day tickets to senior citizens, some active duty military personnel and full-time students. It's best to call the box offices in advance and be prepared to show ID at the box office.

ELECTRICITY
Voltage in the US is 120 volts AC, 60 Hz. Foreign-made appliances may need AC adapters and North American flat-blade plugs.

MONEY AND CURRENCY EXCHANGE
Visitors can exchange currency at banks in central DC, as well as at **Travelex** (1800 K St. NW; 202-872-1428) or **American Express**

Travel Service (1501 K St. NW; 202-457-1300). To report a lost or stolen credit card: American Express (800-528-4800); Diners Club (800-234-6377); MasterCard (800-307-7309); or Visa (800-336-8472).

OPENING HOURS
Most businesses operate Monday to Friday from 9am–5pm. Banks typically stay open from 9am–4pm Monday to Thursday and have extended Friday hours. Some banks offer limited Saturday hours. Post offices in the District tend to operate from 9am–5pm Monday to Thursday, and many close early on Fridays. A few branches offer Saturday hours. The Union Station Post Office (50 Massachusetts Ave, NE, Washington, DC 20002) opens at 7am Monday to Saturday (closed on Sundays). Call 800-275-8777 for specific locations and hours.

The majority of shopping malls and department stores open at either 10 or 11am during the week and on Saturdays, and at noon on Sundays. Stores tend to close at 8 or 9pm except on Sundays when most shut at 5pm. The majority of retail establishments have extended hours in December. Bars in the District open at 11am and are permitted to serve alcohol until 2am Sunday to Thursday, and until 3am on Fridays and Saturdays.

SMOKING
The vast majority of restaurants and bars in the District and Maryland do not allow smoking. A small number of establishments remain exempt from the ban, which applies to most public indoor spaces. Virginia currently does not have a state-wide smoking ban.

MUST KNOW

SPECTATOR SPORTS

DC is a great place to be a spectator where sports are concerned. The city's major professional sports teams include the Washington Nationals (baseball), the Washington Capitals (hockey), and the Washington Wizards (basketball). A city full of loyal football fans makes Washington Redskins tickets hard to come by if you don't have season tickets. Individual tickets sometimes do show up on eBay or www.craigslist.org.

Nationals Park

On March 30, 2008, a brand new baseball stadium for the Washington Nationals opened in Southeast Washington, a few blocks from the Capitol. Nationals Park (888-632-6287; http://nationals.mlb.com) is in an area currently experiencing tremendous development with plans for restaurants, condos and nightlife underway.

The steel, glass and concrete stadium is the first major US stadium to be accredited as a Leadership in Energy and Environmental Design (LEED) structure. Behind-the-scenes stadium tours are given on non-game days; $15 for adults and $12 for children.

TAXES AND TIPPING

Prices displayed in the US do not include sales tax (5.75% in DC), which is not reimbursable. It's customary to give a small gift of money—a tip—for services rendered, to waiters (15-20% of bill), porters ($1 per bag), chamber maids ($1 per day) and cab drivers (15% of fare).

Spectator Sports			
Sport/Team	Season	Venue	Phone/Website
Baseball (National League) Washington Nationals	Apr–Sept	Nationals Park 1500 S. Capitol St, SE *	Tickets: 888-6326287 www.nationals.mlb.com
Football (NFL) Washington Redskins	Sept–Dec	FedEx Field Landover, MD	Tickets: 301-276-6050 www.redskins.com
Hockey (NHL) Washington Capitals	Oct–Apr	Verizon Center 7th & F Sts. NW	Info: 202-628-3200 Tickets: 202-266-2277 www.washingtoncaps.com
Basketball (NBA) Washington Wizards	Nov–Apr	Verizon Center 7th & F Sts. NW	Info: 202-628-3200 Tickets: 202-661-5050 www.washingtonwizards.com
Basketball (WNBA) Washington Mystics	May–Aug	Verizon Center 7th & F Sts. NW	Info: 202-661-5050 Tickets: 202-266-2277 or 397-7328 www.washingtonmystics.com
Soccer (MLS) DC United	Apr–Oct	RFK Stadium E. Capitol & 22nd Sts. SE	Info: 202-587-5000 Tickets: 202-397-7328 www.dcunited.com

WASHINGTON, DC

This is where it all happens: the political wheeling and dealing, the power lunches, the late-night trysts on the Capitol grounds. Politics rule the day in the nation's capital, where power is king and administrations can rise and fall at the will of the people.

It all started with George Washington in 1790. Elected America's first president after the new nation won its independence from Britain in the Revolutionary War, Washington was charged with finding a suitable place to locate the seat of government. The spot he chose was a tract of land near the prosperous port of Georgetown. Washington knew this area well—his own plantation, Mount Vernon, lay just 16mi south along the Potomac River.

Washington appointed French major Pierre Charles L'Enfant (1754–1825) to design the new capital. L'Enfant, who fought under General Washington in the Revolution, had formal training in architecture and design. The plan conceived by the Frenchman called for a diamond-shaped federal district that measured 10mi long on each side and encompassed portions of Maryland as well as the county of Alexandria on the west bank of the Potomac River.

One of L'Enfant's first decisions was to situate the future "Congress house" on Jenkins Hill, which commanded a striking view of the Potomac River. Along this east–west axis he planned a 400-foot-wide "Grand Avenue" (now The Mall) to be lined by foreign ministries and cultural institutions. The avenue would connect on a north–south axis with the "President's house," which in turn would link back to the Capitol via a mile-long commercial corridor (present-day Pennsylvania Avenue). L'Enfant laid out the rest of the city in a grid pattern of streets intersected by broad diagonal avenues at "round points" (DC's infamous traffic circles).

Despite numerous setbacks, including L'Enfant's dismissal in 1792, Washington was well on its way to

House Chamber, November 17, 1947

Library of Congress

©Ken Cole/Dreamstime.com

Cherry blossoms along the tidal basin

becoming a city by the mid-19C. In 1871 the District of Columbia incorporated Georgetown, and improved transportation-spurred growth in neighboring Virginia and Maryland.

Today the Washington metropolitan area is home to more than a half-million people and fans out into densely settled suburbs reaching north toward Baltimore, Maryland; south toward Alexandria, Virginia; east across the broad estuarine expanse of Maryland's Eastern Shore; and west toward the Blue Ridge Mountains. The rumblings that preceded the Civil War began in the mountains west of Washington in Harpers Ferry, West Virginia *(see Excursions)*. Once the war exploded, some of its most noted battles were fought in the countryside within an hour's drive of the capital.

Conceived as a national showplace, Washington, DC reigns as a truly international city, boasting world-class museums and spectacular memorials, fine performing arts and great shopping and dining. As the political heart of the nation, DC is remarkably accessible, opening the doors of Congress, the Supreme Court and other federal institutions to the visitors who come to witness democracy in action.

A Government For The People

In order to create a system of checks and balances, The US Constitution divides the government into three separate branches—legislative, judicial, and executive. The Executive Branch is headed by the president and vice president—both elected together for a maximum of two four-year terms. The Legislative Branch drafts and passes laws and is made up of two sections, a House of Representatives and a smaller Senate, collectively known as Congress. The smallest of the three branches, the Judicial Branch consists of the US Supreme Court (the country's highest court), some 94 district courts and 13 appellate courts.

POWER AND POLITICS

GOVERNMENT SITES

The nation's capital—the seat of the United States government—is anything but just another tourist site. You can't help but be moved when you see how much larger the Capitol building, the White House, the Memorials and other grand government buildings are when you see them in person. DC is a destination like no other—it's the place where the checks and balances established by the US Constitution still protect the freedoms Americans hold so dear.

Inside the dome, the Capitol

Destination DC

The Capitol★★★

1st St. between Independence & Constitution Aves. NE. 202-225-6827. www.aoc.gov. Open year-round Mon–Sat 9am–4:30pm. Closed Sun, Thanksgiving Day & Dec 25. (Bags larger than 14" wide x 13" high x 4" deep , luggage, food, beverages, knitting needles, non-aerosol spays, cans, bottles,

pointed objects, and weapons are among the long list of items not allowed in building.)

The tiered white dome crowned by the Statue of Freedom is America's Icon of democracy in progress. The design of the massive Capitol building, which has been home to US Congress since 1800, resulted from a public competition held

---

Watching Democracy In Action

The Capitol is open to the public for guided tours only. Visitors must obtain free timed tickets on the day of their visit, beginning at 9am on a first-come, first served basis, at Capitol Guide Service Kiosk (Independence Ave. & 1st St. SW).
The public only has access to the Senate Chambers or the Hall of the House of Representatives when Congress is in session. US citizens can obtain passes to the visitor galleries to view a House or Senate session through the office of their state's senator or representative. Foreign visitors must apply for passes at the South Visitor Receiving Facility (near Independence Ave. SW; foreign photo ID required). Call for schedule and agenda: 202-224-8601 or 202-224-3121.

by President George Washington and Secretary of State Thomas Jefferson. The winner, Dr. William Thornton, was awarded $500 and a city lot. The cornerstone was laid in 1793, and by 1800 Congress was able to leave Philadelphia—the young republic's temporary capital—and take up residence in the new federal city.

Following Thornton's resignation in the early 1800s, the Capitol was completed over the next 30-odd years with the help of architects Benjamin Latrobe and Charles Bulfinch. The building was expanded in the mid-19C by Thomas U. Walter; a hundred years later, Congress had outgrown the Capitol again, and the east facade was extended.

Great Rotunda – The ornate Capitol **dome★★**, 180 feet high and 90 feet across, displays an allegorical fresco, *The Apotheosis of Washington*, by Constantino Brumidi.

Main Floor – Semicircular half-domed Statuary Hall appears (unfurnished) as it did in 1857 when it served as the House Chamber.

Old Senate Chamber – The Supreme Court held sway here from 1860 to 1935.

Ground Floor – Arched ceilings and walls of the intersecting **Brumidi Corridors** are decorated with Brumidi's murals.

On December 2, 2008, The Capitol Visitor Center opens to the public The long-awaited visitor's center houses an exhibition gallery, orientation theaters, a 530-seat cafeteria, gift shops, and restrooms. Visit www.aoc.go for more information about the center.

The White House★★★

1600 Pennsylvania Ave. NW. 202-208-1631. www.whitehouse.gov. Visit by guided tour only. Closed Sun & Mon and federal holidays. No individual tours; groups of 10 or more may schedule tours up to 6 months in advance. Call the 24-hour visitor information line: 202-456-7041.

What American hasn't dreamed of living at the White House? Universal symbol of the US presidency,

©PhotoDisc
White House

Visiting the White House

- **First Floor** Contains formal state reception areas.
- **East Room** Hosts concerts, dances and official White House ceremonies.
- **Green Room** The drawing room boasts green watered-silk wall coverings and furniture from the 19C workshop of Duncan Phyfe.
- **Blue Room** This elliptical room includes seven of the original Bellange gilded armchairs ordered from Paris by James Monroe.
- **State Dining Room** The site of official dinners seats 140.
- **Second & Third Floors** These floors contain the First Family's living quarters.
- **West Wing** *Not open to the public.* Houses the Cabinet Room, staff and reception rooms, and the President's Oval Office.

this Georgian beauty has housed America's presidents and their families, beginning with John Adams in 1801.

A public contest was held in 1792 to find someone to design the "president's palace" (as DC planner Pierre L'Enfant called it), which today is surrounded by 18 acres of green lawns and flower gardens. Even Thomas Jefferson, a self-taught architect, submitted an entry—anonymously.

Jefferson lost the competition, and the $500 prize went instead to a young Irish builder, James Hoban. Although the cornerstone was set in 1792, the house was not completed during President Washington's term in office. So John Adams, the nation's second president, became the first to live in the whitewashed stone mansion.

When James Madison lived here as the fourth president of the US, the British set fire to the White House during the War of 1812. Fortunately, a well-timed rain saved the house from burning to the ground. Over the years, the Executive Mansion has been expanded and redecorated, reflecting the tastes of the First Families who have occupied it for more than 200 years.

Department of State Diplomatic Reception Rooms★★

23rd St. between C & D Sts. NW. 202-647-3241. www.state.gov. Visit by prearranged guided tour only, year-round Mon–Fri 9:30am, 10:30am & 2:45pm. Make reservations four weeks in advance. Closed weekends & major holidays. Tour is not recommended for children under 12.

To look at the main State Department office building, you'd never guess that inside this undistinguished 1960s structure hide masterpieces of 18C interior design. Used for official functions

---

Tips For Visiting

The White House Visitor Center *(SE corner of 15th & E Sts.; open daily 7:30am–4pm)* complements a tour with exhibits on various aspects of the White House.

Best Rooms in the House

(Diplomatic Reception Rooms are located on the 8th floor)

- **Edward Vason Jones Memorial Hall** This elegant foyer is appointed with faux marble pilasters and cornices, and gray marble floors.
- **Entrance Hall** Adjoining Memorial Hall, the Entrance Hall contains the oldest dated and signed piece of furniture in North America; it was made by Benjamin Frothingham of Charlestown, Massachusetts in 1753.
- **John Quincy Adams State Drawing Room** The secretary of State greets official guests in this 18C-style drawing room, with its hand-carved architectural details. Here you'll find the English Sheraton desk where John Jay signed the Treaty of Paris in 1783.
- **Thomas Jefferson State Reception Room** The perfect Neoclassical proportions of the State Reception Room reflect Jefferson's own architectural tastes.
- **Benjamin Franklin State Dining Room** Largest of the Diplomatic Reception Rooms, the ornate State Dining Room was redesigned by John Blatteau in 1985 with red-veined scagliola marble columns running the length of the room. An 8,000-pound Savonnerie rug covers the floor; on the ceiling, eight cut-glass chandeliers flank the Great Seal of the US, fashioned in plaster and gilt.

hosted by the secretary of State and other high-level government officials, the Diplomatic Reception Rooms are furnished with one of the country's most impressive collections of 18C **American decorative arts★★** dating from 1750 to 1825.

When the State Department headquarters building opened in 1961, its eighth-floor reception rooms were furnished in a stark, streamlined decor in keeping with the building's concrete-and-glass modernism.

Shortly thereafter, the Americana Project, under the direction of the Fine Arts Committee of the State Department, was begun to upgrade these areas through private donations.

Georgia architect Edward Vason Jones dedicated the last 15 years of his life to redesigning the rooms in the style of great 18C American manor houses.

Library of Congress★★

1st St. & Independence Ave. SE. 202-707-5000. Hours of operation 202-707-6400 www.loc.gov. Thomas Jefferson Building open year-round Mon–Sat 10am–5pm. Call for reading room hours—they vary among the 21 reading room in the Thomas Jefferson, James Madison and John Adams buildings. For exhibition information call 202-707-4604. All library buildings closed Sun & major holidays.

Imagine the largest library in existence, then double it, and you've got the Library of Congress. Its collection numbers a mind-boggling 138 million items and counting—enough to keep even the most devoted bibliophile happy for several lifetimes. Established in 1800 (and housed in the Capitol) for the exclusive use of Congress, the library became a public institution in 1864 under

A Library For The People

The Library of Congress is open to the general public and functions as a reference library for individuals 16 years or older. Researchers must register in Room 140 of the James Madison Building. An orientation video is shown regularly in the visitor center *(ground floor, Jefferson Bldg.)*.

Free guided tours of the Jefferson Building are available. A cafeteria *(open for lunch)* is located on the 6th floor of the Madison Building. For visitor information or assistance in using the research facilities, consult the touch-screen terminals in the visitor center.

Visitor information – 202-707-8000   **Research information** – 202-707-6500
Tour information – 202-707-9779

the direction of Librarian of Congress Ainsworth Rand Spofford. A separate building—now known as the **Thomas Jefferson Building**★★—for the library opened in 1897; it has served as the "national library of the United States" ever since. A richly ornamented Beaux-Arts-style landmark, the Jefferson Building fills an entire square block across from the Capitol. Together with the 1939 Art Deco **John Adams Building** *(2nd St. SE, behind the main building)* and the austere 1980 **James Madison Memorial Building** *(Independence Ave., between 1st & 2nd Sts. SE)*, the three structures that make up the Library of Congress hold more than 20 million books, 61 million manuscripts, 5 million maps and atlases, and 5 million pieces of sheet music.

Great Hall – The Jefferson Building's two-story Great Hall is noted for its gold-leaf ceiling and vaulted corridors. Here you'll find a copy of the mid-15C Giant Bible of Mainz—one of the last hand-illuminated manuscript versions of the Bible.

Main Reading Room – An elaborately sculpted grand staircase leads to the second-story colonnade, where a visitors' gallery overlooks the Main Reading Room—a vast rotunda under the library's massive copper dome. The room is ringed by Corinthian columns and

Great Hall, Jefferson Building, Library of Congress

Library of Congress

Supreme Court

Brigitta L. House/Michelin

arched windows with stained-glass state seals and eagles.

Supreme Court★★

1st & E. Capitol Sts. NE. 202-479-3211. www.supremecourtus.gov. Open year-round daily 9am–4:30pm. Closed weekends & major holidays.

Located across the street from the Capitol is the highest court in the land. The Court was established by Article III of the US Constitution, ratified in 1788, which called for a "supreme court" to have the final decision in matters of law and to act as a counterbalance to the legislative and executive branches of government. In 1790 the first US Supreme Court met at the Royal Exchange Building in the temporary capital of New York City. In 1800 it moved to DC and occupied several different rooms in the Capitol over the years. William Howard Taft, the tenth chief justice (1921–1930) and the only US president to serve on the Court, convinced Congress in 1828 to set aside funds for a building to house the Court. More than a century later (October 1935), the present cross-shaped marble structure, designed by Cass Gilbert, was completed.

Nine justices, who are appointed by the president with Senate approval, serve on the Supreme Court. Only death, voluntary retirement or resignation, or congressional impeachment can remove a sitting justice.

Justice For All

The Court's term begins on the first Monday in October. From October through April the Court hears oral arguments on cases it has agreed to review. Of the 7,000-some requests for review it receives annually, the Court hears only 75–100 cases. Judges typically sit for two weeks a month *(Mon–Wed)*. From mid-May through June the Court convenes on Monday to deliver its opinions on cases argued during that term. Court sessions are open to the public on a first-come, first-served basis. Check the Washington Post for the daily schedule of hearings.

Best of the Supreme Court Building

- Two James Fraser sculptures, representing the Contemplation of Justice (left) and the Authority of Law (right), flank the broad staircase in front of the Supreme Court.
- Within the huge courtroom chamber, justices sit on a raised bench ringed by massive columns. The justices' places are ordered by their seniority, with the chief justice taking the center position.
- A statue of **John Marshall** (1755–1835), the "Great Chief Justice" who held the post from 1801–1835, dominates the main hall on the ground level.

Bureau of Engraving and Printing★

14th & C Sts. SW. 202-874-2330. www.moneyfactory.com. Visit by guided tour only May–Aug Mon–Fri 9am–10:45am, 12:30pm–2pm & 5pm–7pm. Rest of year Mon–Fri 10am–2pm. Closed weekends & major holidays. The building also is closed when the Department of Homeland Security threat level is elevated to Code Orange (check www.dhs.gov for current level).

If you get a thrill from being surrounded by money, this is the place to be. "The nation's money factory" produces US paper currency and many of the official documents issued by the US government. Located at the foot of the 14th Street Bridge, the Bureau of Engraving and Printing turns out 37 million notes a day with a face value of approximately $696 million.

The entrance hall contains displays and a 15-minute film on the history of US paper-money production. The remainder of the tour leads past three processing rooms, and ends in an exhibit hall displaying stamps, bills and historical documents. From May–Sept visitors must obtain same-day, free tour tickets from the kiosk on the bureau's 15th Street side, beginning at 8am.

Old Post Office

Pennsylvania Ave. & 12th St. NW. 202-289-4224. www.oldpostoffice dc.com. Tower open Mon–Sat 9am–5pm, Sun 10am–5pm. From Jun 1 until Labor Day the Tower stays open until 8pm. Free Clock Tower tours are given every five minutes. Pavillion Hours: Mon–Sat, 10 am–8 pm and Sun 12pm–7pm (Mar–Aug); Mon–Sat, 10am–7pm and Sun 12pm–6pm (Sept–Feb.) Call 202-606-8691 for more information. Closed Jan 1, Thanksgiving Day & Dec 25.

The Color of Money

Green ink was chosen for one side of America's original paper currency because of its resistance to physical and chemical change, earning these early notes the name "greenbacks." In 2003 the Bureau of Engraving and Printing together with the Federal Reserve introduced redesigned notes. The new notes, which are intended to deter counterfeiters, use color-shifting ink that changes its hue when the note is tilted.

This Pennsylvania Avenue landmark is lucky to still be around. When it was completed in 1899 as the headquarters of the US Postal Service and the city's first skyscraper, many people didn't like the way it looked. The massive granite Post Office with its rough-faced masonry and corner turrets, was nicknamed "Old Tooth" for the 315-foot tower that stuck out above the rest of the structure. Designed in the Richardsonian Romanesque style, the Post Office didn't match the Neoclassical architecture that was popular in DC at the time. It was saved from the wrecker's ball at the eleventh hour and converted into a multifunctional complex with office and commercial space. Today the **Old Post Office Pavilion** and its shops and eateries attract residents and tourists alike throughout the year.

Pavilion – The first three levels of the central glass-roofed courtyard teem with stores, restaurants, a food court, and a stage for live entertainment.

Tower – From the observation deck at the top of the clock tower you'll have a great **view** of DC *(take the glass elevator from the courtyard)*. Near the summit are the 10 **Congress bells** that are played to mark the opening and closing sessions of Congress.

The Ronald Reagan Building and International Trade Center

1300 Pennsylvania Ave NW. www.itcdc.com. Free tours of the building given on Mon, Wed, and Fri at 11am. Mar 14–Labor Day open from 8:30am–5pm during the week, 9am–4pm on Sat and closed on Sun. Rest of the year 9am–4:30pm and closed Sat and Sun.

When you first see the massive Ronald Reagan Building it's hard to picture the eyesore of a parking lot that once stood on this prime piece of real estate for more than 50 years. The 3.1-million-square-foot structure that now occupies the spot is the first federal building to be designed for both government and private use and the largest federal building to be constructed in the area since the Pentagon. Public art adorns both the inside and outside of the building, including a huge neon and glass sculpture in the atrium, a section of the Berlin Wall on the ground level and the bronze Bearing Witness sculpture outside in the plaza. The Ronald Reagan Building and International Trade Center and also houses the Washington DC Visitor Information Center *(www.dcchamber.org or 202-289-8317)*.

The Pentagon

703-697-1776. http://pentagon.afis.osd.mil. Tours Mon–Fri 9am–3pm (minimun 5 people) must be requested in advance and photo ID must be shown.
The heart of the American military establishment, this enormous pentagonal building houses the offices of the highest authorities of the armed services. Each of its five sides is larger than the Capitol, and together they contain 17½ miles of corridors. Some 23,000 personnel work here in round the clock shifts.

MUSEUMS

You may groan when you hear the word "museums," but with choices from art to zoology—and everything in between—DC's museum offerings are bound to please even the most hardened culture-phobe. The capital's cultural heart and the world's densest concentration of museums lie along the east end of the **National Mall★★★**, the mile-long, tree-lined esplanade extending from the foot of Capitol Hill to 15th Street. Here you'll find the many museums of the **Smithsonian Institution** *(no admission fee)*, established in 1846 with an endowment from prominent English scientist James Smithson.

National Air and Space Museum★★★

6th St. at Independence Ave. SW. 202-633-1000. www.nasm. si.edu. Open year-round daily 10am–5:30pm. Extended Summer Hours from May 23–Aug 31, 10am–7:30pm. Closed Dec 25.

Who hasn't dreamed they could fly? From the Wright Brothers' *1903 Flyer* to John Glenn's space capsule *Friendship 7*, the milestones of man's fascination with flight are presented here at the world's most visited museum. Established in 1946 to "memorialize the national development of aviation," the National Air and Space Museum (NASM) contains the world's most comprehensive collection of aircraft, spacecraft and flight-related artifacts. Architect Gyo Obata designed the Tennessee-marble-faced structure that opened for the nation's bicentennial in July 1976. The 22 galleries within the building's four massive rectangles contain hundreds of aircraft and spacecraft, rockets, guided missiles and satellites, as well as exhibits that trace the history of flight from its earliest days through World War II and into the space age. Be sure to try your hand **At the Controls of Flight Simulator Zone**, where you can execute gut-wrenching aerobatics aboard the MaxFlight® RS2000 simulator. Don't leave without a virtual soar through the sky in NASM's classic movie *To Fly* shown

America by Air

Photo by Eric Long, National Air and Space Museum, Smithsonian Institution

MUST SEE

Spacesuits of Neil Armstrong and Buzz Aldrin

Photo by Eric Long, National Air and Space Museum, Smithsonian Institution

on the five-story screen of the Lockheed Martin IMAX® Theater.

Milestones of Flight –
Occupying the central part of the building, this hall displays such epoch-making aircraft as Charles Lindbergh's Ryan NYP, *Spirit of St. Louis*, and Chuck Yeager's Bell X-1, *Glamorous Glennis*.

America by Air – The museum's newest permanent gallery, tells the story of passenger air travel in the United States, from the early attempts to form airlines only a decade after Kitty Hawk to the commercial challenges and technical sophistication of the 21st-century jet age.

Visitors can see seven complete airplanes from the early years of aviation; experience the Jet Set era inside the front section and cockpit of a real Boeing 747; initiate a realistic take-off from the pilot's seat of an Airbus A320; and feel what it was like to fly on a noisy, vibrating 1930s Ford TriMotor.

Explore The Universe –
The museum's newest permanent exhibit explores four centuries of human observations of the galaxies, and showcases astronomers' tools from early astrolabes to the Hubble Space Telescope.

How Things Fly – This area includes exhibits on gravity and air, stability and control and other principles of flight. Visitors can man the controls of a Cessna 150 or activate a supersonic wind tunnel.

Space Hall – Large rockets, guided missiles and manned spacecraft are featured here. On display are a model of the Columbia space shuttle as well as the Apollo-Soyuz spacecraft, which was used for a joint docking-in-space experiment with the Russians in the 1970s.

Early 20C: Flight Takes Off

1903 – Wilbur and Orville Wright make the first successful motorized flight at Kitty Hawk, North Carolina, in their *1903 Flyer*.

1909 – Louis Blériot crosses the English Channel in 36 minutes in a Type XI monoplane.

1911 – G.P. Rodgers makes the first coast-to-coast flight in the Dutch-built Fokker T-2.

1927 – Charles Lindbergh makes the first solo non-stop crossing of the Atlanti

1932 – Amelia Earhart becomes the first woman to make a solo nonstop trans-atlantic flight.

1947 – Air Force pilot Chuck Yeager breaks the sound barrier in his Bell X-1.

National Gallery of Art★★★

Madison Dr., between 3rd & 7th Sts. NW. 202-737-4215. www.nga.gov. Open year-round Mon–Sat 10am–5pm, Sun 11am–6pm. Closed Jan 1 & Dec 25. Sections of the National Gallery may be closed for renovation.

You'll want to make a beeline for this place if art is your passion. Even if it's not, you're bound to find something you like among the more than 116,000 paintings, drawings, prints, photographs, sculpture, and decorative arts pieces. A world-class art institution, the National Gallery traces the development of Western art from the Middle Ages to the present. Its holdings have mushroomed from a core of 126 paintings and a group of fine 15C–16C Italian sculptures displayed in the stately marble West Building (1941) that graces the Mall; today gallery operations are supported by federal monies.

West Building – Renowned architect John Russell Pope designed this domed Classical Revival structure, the exterior of which glows with seven shades of pink Tennessee marble. Arranged in chronological order, galleries on the main floor of the West Building progress from a superb group of 13C–15C Italian paintings through Spanish, German and Flemish masterpieces to 19C French paintings. Works by Thomas Gainsborough and J.M.W. Turner are included among the collection of British Paintings, while the portraiture of Benjamin West, Charles Willson Peale and Gilbert Stuart highlight the American Painting galleries.

East Building★★ – In the 1970s the Mellon family again came forward to endow the museum's acclaimed East Building (1978, I.M. Pei), which is devoted to late-19C and 20C art. Considered the most impressive example of modern architecture in Washington, the East Building *(entrance on 4th St. across the plaza from the West Building)* opens into a soaring skylit atrium dominated by an im-

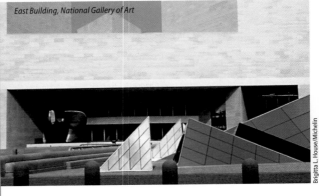

East Building, National Gallery of Art

Brigitta L. House/Michelin

Micro Visit

A trip to the immense NGA can be daunting, but a few minutes spent at the museum's **Micro Gallery** can help simplify your visit. Located in the art information room *(to the left of the main entrance)*, the Micro Gallery is an interactive computer system that allows visitors to explore more than 1,500 works of art from the museum's permanent collection using touch-screen monitors. Orient yourself to the museum with maps and practical information; survey the life and work of more than 650 artists; view the museum catalog; or create a personal tour of works you want to see, complete with printed maps showing their location.

mense red, blue and black mobile by Alexander Calder, which was specially commissioned for this space. Five floors of open, fluid gallery space showcase the work of Pablo Picasso, Wassily Kandinsky, Mark Rothko and Georgia O'Keeffe, among others.

National Gallery of Art Sculpture Garden – *On the Mall at 7th St. & Constitution Ave. NW.* This six-acre urban oasis is filled with trees, flowerbeds and contemporary sculptures by the likes of Alexander Calder, Claes Oldenburg and Joan Miró. In winter, the garden's reflecting pool, with its dramatic circular fountain, doubles as an ice-skating rink *(see Musts for Fun)*.

Arthur M. Sackler Gallery★★

The Smithsonian Quadrangle at 1050 Independence Ave. SW. 202-633-4880. www.asia.si.edu. Open year-round daily 10am–5:30pm. Closed Dec 25. An underground gallery links the Sackler to the adjacent Freer Gallery, with which it's closely associated.

If your tastes run more toward ancient than modern art, then you'll enjoy the Sackler, which is dedicated to the study and exhibition of the arts of Asia from the Neolithic period to the present. The gallery's major strengths are in Chinese jades and bronzes, ancient Near Eastern gold and silverwork and a collection of 11C–19C

Jade chimera with rider, (c. 25-220), Eastern Han dynasty, Arthur Sackler Gallery

Arthur Sackler Gallery

MUSEUMS

Chinese Art Unraveled

Ancient Chinese culture placed particular importance on tradition: Laws and customs were passed down through the generations, and ancestor worship was a common practice. This is why ancestral figures often decorate ritual bronzes and jades. The economy was largely agricultural, and the elements of nature became a powerful force in ancient Chinese religion. Clouds, rain, wind and stars appear frequently as symbols on vessels and other objects, which the Chinese used to ward off evil spirits and to ask for the protection of their gods.

Islamic manuscripts. The core of the museum's holdings was a gift from **Dr. Arthur M. Sackler** (1913–1987), the New York psychiatrist, medical researcher and publisher who donated 1,000 objects from his personal collection to the Smithsonian Institution in 1982.

Jade Collection – The mountains of the Chinese provinces contained rich veins of nephrite jade, a gemstone so prized by the Chinese that they associate it with the five cardinal virtues: charity, modesty, courage, justice and wisdom. The Sackler has a jade collection of more than 450 decorated objects dating back to 3000 BC.

Chinese Bronzes – The gallery's bronzes date from the Shang through the Han dynasties (1700 BC–AD 220). Many of these objects have lengthy inscriptions, which provide a wealth of information about this period.

Ancient Near Eastern Gold and Silver – The civilizations that developed in ancient Iran, Anatolia (present-day Turkey) and the region around the Caucasus Mountains are credited with introducing metalwork as early as 7000 BC. Over the centuries, the craftspeople of these regions made exquisite objects in copper, silver, gold and lead. Many of the gold and silver ceremonial vessels and ornaments in the Sackler collection date from 3000 BC to the 8C AD.

Corcoran Gallery★★

500 17th St, 17th St & New York Ave, NW. 202-639-1700. www.corcoran.org. Open year-round daily 10am–5pm and Thu until 9pm. Closed Mon and Tue and Jan 1 & Dec 25. $6.

Just a hop, skip and a jump from the White House *(one block southwest)* is the largest non-federal art museum in DC. Counting more than 14,000 works in its permanent holdings, the Corcoran showcases a collection of European and American art, as well as a renowned group of 20C American paintings, sculpture and

Raising the Roof

Restoration and renovation on the Corcoran's Beaux-Arts facade and roof is currently underway. Exhibitions will continue as planned, and the building will remain open to the public during the work, which is scheduled to be completed in fall 2010.

Corcoran Gallery of Art

Detail of Into Bondage (1936) by Aaron Douglas

photography, arranged around a skylit two-story atrium.

Self-made man and respected philanthropist, **William Wilson Corcoran** (1798–1888) began constructing a museum to house his private art collection in 1859. That building—now the Renwick Gallery *(see p 52)*—was almost complete when Corcoran halted the project in 1861. A Southern sympathizer, Corcoran found himself unwelcome in Civil War-era Washington, and he left for Europe in 1862. When he returned after the war, Corcoran resumed his museum project.

In 1870 he donated his personal collection, the building and grounds, and a $900,000 endowment to be used "for the purpose of encouraging American genius." One of the nation's first major art galleries, the Corcoran, opened in 1874.

By 1897 the collection had outgrown the space, and the elegant white-marble Beaux-Arts structure (designed by Ernest Flagg) that now houses the museum opened several blocks south of the old building. Above the new museum's entrance is its motto: "Dedicated to Art."

In 1925 Sen. William Andrew Clark of Montana gave the Corcoran his noted collection of works by such masters as Rembrandt, Turner, and Degas. The Clark Bequest also included the **Salon Doré**, an 18C Parisian salon appointed with gilded woodwork, moldings and paneling.

Four Centuries of Art

The major schools of art represented at the Corcoran:

- **French Impressionism** – Renoir, Pissarro, Monet
- **Hudson River School** – Thomas Cole, Frederic Church, Albert Bierstadt
- **African-American Art** – Aaron Douglas, Henry O. Tanner, Raymond Saunders
- **Abstract Expressionism** – Hans Hofmann, Mark Rothko, Helen Frankenthaler

MUSEUMS

35

Freer Gallery★★

Jefferson Dr. at 12th St. SW. 202-633.4880. www.asia.si.edu. Open year-round daily 10am–5:30pm. Closed Dec 25. An underground exhibition gallery connects the Freer and the Sackler Gallery.

If Asian art is your thing, the Freer is for you. First of the Smithsonian museums on the Mall devoted exclusively to art, the Freer Gallery possesses an outstanding Asian collection as well as one of the world's largest collections of works by **James McNeill Whistler** (1834–1903). The marble and granite Renaissance-style structure, which incorporates a central courtyard, was officially opened in 1923. Wealthy railroad-car manufacturer **Charles L. Freer** (1854–1919) became a keen collector of Asian art. From his first purchase of a Japanese fan in 1887, he gradually amassed thousands of objects. He also bought several Whistler prints in 1887, his initial purchase of works by the artist who would become his good friend. In 1904 Freer revealed plans to bequeath a significant portion of his collections to the Smithsonian Institution and to finance the construction of a building to house the art. From that original gift of some 9,000 works, the museum's Asian holdings have grown to over 27,000 objects (Freer requested that his American collection not be expanded).

Chinese Collection –
These works include ornamental implements of the emperors of the Ming (1368–1644) and Qing (1644–1911) dynasties, 15C blue-and-white porcelain bowls from the Imperial workshop in southeast China, and one of the world's finest collections of ancient bronzes, jades and laquerware.

Japanese Collection –
Spanning 4,000 years, the collection of Japanese art highlights hanging scrolls, 15C–19C byobu, or folding screens, ceramics and lacquered wooden boxes (late-16C–19C), and 13C–17C stone and earthenware tea bowls.
Korean ceramics (10C–14C), Indian court paintings (16C–19C), and Islamic manuscripts round out the Asian holdings.

Harmony in blue and gold: The Peacock Room by James McNeill Whistler

Courtesy of Freer Gallery of Art, Smithsonian Institution/ John Tsantes and Jeffery Crespi

Whistler's Works

Of special interest among the American works are Whistler's "Notes," miniature oils depicting English landscapes c. 1882; and "Nocturnes," dramatic paintings of the Thames River at night. The **Peacock Room★**, Whistler's only existing interior design (1876–77), is permanently installed in Gallery 12. An overhaul of English shipping tycoon Frederick Leyland's London dining room, Whistler's design provides a sumptuous gilded setting for Leyland's collection of blue-and-white Chinese porcelain.

Hillwood Museum and Gardens★★

Hillwood Gardens

Brigitta L. House/Michelin

4155 Linnean Ave. NW. 202-686-5807. www.hillwoodmuseum.org. Reservations strongly encouraged from late Mar–May. Open year-round Tue–Sat 10am–5pm. Closed Mon, Jan, major holidays and most Sundays. $12.

Cereals and czars might sound like an odd combination, but they both played a key role in the life of businesswoman **Marjorie Merriweather Post** (1887–1973). As heiress to the Post cereal fortune, Post owed her wealth to, well, corn flakes. Her money helped buy fine pieces of art that once belonged to Russia's czars. Today you can see Post's remarkable collection of **Russian decorative arts★★★**—the most extensive of its kind outside Russia—in her columned brick mansion that looks down on Rock Creek Park.

A Gambol on the Grounds

Outside, you can wander wooded paths that connect a host of gardens, including a formal French parterre hedged by boxwoods, a rose garden encircling a monument marking Mrs. Post's grave, and a Japanese-style garden where waterfalls cascade through a series of ponds.

In the late 1930s Marjorie Post travelled with her third husband, Joseph E. Davies, to Moscow, where he served as ambassador from 1937–38. The timing was perfect. About that time, the Soviet government began selling art that had been confiscated from the Imperial family, members of the aristocracy and the Russian Orthodox Church during the Revolution of 1917. The treasures Post and her husband collected illustrate more than 200 years of Russian decorative arts, from the reign of Peter the Great (1682–1725) to the days of the last czar, Nicholas II (1868–1918), when jeweler Carl Fabergé created his fabulous Easter eggs for the Russian royal family.

Reopened in fall 2000 after a three-year renovation, Hillwood is filled with 18C and 19C French furnishings that reflect the elegance of the estate during the time Mrs. Post lived there (1955–1973).

Icon Room★★ – Here you'll find Post's finest Fabergé pieces, including two (of the more than 50) Imperial Easter eggs that he crafted, as well as a diamond nuptial crown worn by Alexandra at her 1894 wedding to Nicholas II.

Dining Room – The exquisite inlaid-marble Florentine table seats 30 guests.

French Drawing Room – This room is decked out in the ornate Louis XVI style.

Russian Porcelain Room – Dinnerware commissioned by Catherine the Great is show-cased here.

Hirshhorn Museum★★

Independence Ave. at 7th St. SW. 202-633-1000. http://hirshhorn. si.edu. Open year-round daily 10am–5:30pm. Closed Dec 25.

Hirshhorn Museum and Sculpture Garden

Smithsonian Institution/Destination DC

You'd never guess that this unadorned concrete "doughnut" (1966, Gordon Bunshaft) on the Mall houses one of the finest collections of modern art in the country. Elevated on four piers, the drum-shaped building wraps around a fountain plaza that ex-tends beneath the raised building.

Sculptures here, which range from the realistic to the monumental and abstract, make up the world's most comprehensive collection of 20C works. The Hirshhorn also claims one of the country's most extensive collections of works by celebrated British sculptor **Henry Moore** (1898–1986).

Born in Latvia, **Joseph Hirshhorn** (1899–1981) immigrated to Brooklyn with his widowed mother and 10 siblings when he was six years old. He eventually became a wealthy financier and turned his attention to collecting art. In the mid-1960s, President Johnson and Smithsonian secretary S. Dillon Ripley convinced Hirshhorn to donate his collection of more than 6,000 works to the Smithsonian. In 1966 Congress established the Hirshhorn Museum and Sculpture Garden. In his will, Hirshhorn left another 6,000 works to the museum. Some 5,000 paintings, 3,000 pieces of sculpture and mixed media and 4,000 works on paper compose the permanent collection, roughly five percent of which is on view in the museum's three levels at any one time.

Third Floor – Paintings are grouped by art movements and organized chronologically, begin-ning with 20C American works (George Bellows, Marsden Hartley, Mark Rothko, Georgia O'Keeffe).

Second Floor – Outer-ring galler-ies here are reserved for temporary exhibits. On the second and third floors, interior galleries feature small sculptural works by the likes of Matisse, Maillol, Rodin, Degas, Picasso and Giacometti.

MUST SEE

Outdoor Sculpture

The plaza on which the building stands was redesigned in 1991 to create outdoor "rooms" for displaying monumental contemporary sculpture, including works by Alexander Calder, Claes Oldenburg and Juan Muñoz. Smaller figurative works are featured in the sunken and walled **Sculpture Garden** *(on the Mall between the Washington Monument and the Capitol).* Here you'll find sculptures by Auguste Rodin, Alexander Calder, Henry Moore and Barbara Hepworth.

First Floor – Focuses on changing exhibits from the permanent collection.

National Archives★★

Constitution Ave., between 7th & 9th Sts. NW. 866-272-6272. www.archives.gov. Open year-round daily 10am–5:30pm (extended hours mid-Mar–Labor Day). Closed Thanksgiving Day & Dec 25.

Are you hankering to read Commodore Matthew Perry's journals from his historic 19C mission to Japan? Have you always wanted to see Mathew Brady's Civil War photographs or the photo albums of Hitler's mistress, Eva Braun? If so, you've come to the right place. An imposing Classical Revival building designed by John Russell Pope, the National Archives and Records Administration—as it is

officially designated—safeguards 5 billion paper documents, 9 million aerial photographs, 6 million still photographs and 300,000 video, film and sound recordings. Completed in 1937, the National Archives filled a pressing need for a central fireproof repository of official and historical records. Before this institution was established, each department of the federal government stored its own archival material, and important documents were frequently lost or damaged.

Rotunda Revisited – Reopened in September 2003 after an extensive renovation, the Rotunda inspires reverence with its 75-foot-high, half-domed space. The centerpiece is a marble dais where the nation's most revered documents are permanently

National Archives

©Cheng Chang/iStockphoto.com

MUSEUMS

Research Facilities

Enter from Pennsylvania Ave. Photo ID required. Children under 16 must be accompanied by an adult. 202-501-5400.

If you're doing scholarly research, head for the ornately paneled **Central Research Room** *(2nd floor)*. Among the holdings here are the papers of the Continental Congress, congressional records and historic correspondence. If you want to trace your family tree, the **Microfilm Research Room** *(4th floor)* is the place to go. It contains census information, military service records, and ship-passenger arrival lists. Staff members are available on-site to provide information about how to research your family history.

enshrined. Sealed in new cases, the **Charters of Freedom★★★** consist of the Declaration of Independence, the Constitution and the Bill of Rights. The renovation made it possible to display all four pages of the Constitution for the first time in history. Fourteen other cases display historical documents relating to the development of the Charters. In fall 2004 the Archives opened a new permanent exhibit, The Public Vaults, as well as a learning center and a 275-seat theater.

National Museum of African Art★★

950 Independence Ave. SW. 202-633-4600. http://africa.si.edu. Open year-round daily 10am–5:30pm. Closed Dec 25.

Come unravel the mystery and magic behind African art at this museum. Devoted to the

Mask (Pwo), Chokwe Peoples, Democratic Republic of Congo

Franko Khoury/National Museum of African Art, Smithsonian Institution

research, acquisition and display of traditional African arts—especially those of the sub-Saharan regions—the museum owns a permanent collection numbering more than 7,000 items. Originally located in a row of Capitol Hill

Out of Africa

Given the pervasive role of religion in African culture, most objects created for utilitarian, economic, aesthetic or ritual purposes are loaded with religious significance. Unlike most cultures throughout the world, which keep written documents, many African cultures rely on sculptured works and other artifacts to pass down values and beliefs from generation to generation. These objects are generally infused with symbolic meanings. An enlarged head, for example, represents power and wisdom.

town houses, the National Museum of African Art now occupies more spacious quarters in the underground Smithsonian Gardens complex on the Mall. Pieces in bronze, copper, wood, ivory and fiber from the permanent collection are rotated among the permanent exhibits here. Throughout the galleries, you'll also find traditional and contemporary African ceramics. Temporary exhibits of African art are arranged from private and public collections, both in the US and abroad.

Images of Power and Identity – Initiation masks, fertility icons, medicinal figurines and other ritual objects are organized by region, emphasizing how geography determines what an object will be made of, as well as its form and style.

Ancient Benin – The museum's holdings of art from the ancient West African kingdom of Benin (present-day Nigeria) include several cast-copper alloy sculptures. Ceremonial figures, heads, pendants and plaques were created between the 15th century and 19th century and reveal the elaborate rituals and ornate regalia worn by the Benin oba (king) before British colonial rule.

Art of the Personal Object – This part of the collection illustrates the beauty and tremendous diversity of design present in everyday objects.

National Museum of American History★★

Constitution Ave., between 12th & 14th Sts. NW. 202-633-1000. http://americanhistory.si.edu. Open year-round daily 10am–5:30pm. Closed Dec 25.

Where else but at the "nation's attic" can you see such national icons as the Star-Spangled Banner, Julia Child's kitchen, and a 1926 Model T Ford? The National Museum of American History's exhibits capture the essence of America's social, political, cultural and scientific development and they explore key events in the nation's past.

Totaling some three million objects, the museum's collection dates back to 1858, when models from the US Patent Office were transferred to the Smithsonian Institution. The current marble structure opened in 1964 as the National Museum of History and Technology; it was renamed the in 1980. Recently the museum completed a two-year renovation of the building's center core, transforming the museum's architectural

NMAH Landmark Objects

As part of the museum's redesign, six iconic American objects now sit in front of each exhibition wing. The artifacts highlight key themes of the exhibitions in that wing and make for great meeting spots for groups.

The six objects are the John Bull steam locomotive, the Vassar Telescope, the Greensboro lunch counter, the George Washington Centennial Statue, Clara Barton's Red Cross ambulance, and a car from Disney's Dumbo the Flying Elephant Ride.

MUSEUMS

appeal while reorganizing and renewing the presentation of its extensive collections. Visitors now enter a dramatic five-story sky-lit atrium, surrounded by displays. An architectural representation of a waving flag—960 reflective tiles —frames the entrance to the new Star-Spangled Banner gallery. And, a grand staircase now links the museum's first and second floors.

First Floor – Discover the extent to which transportation and power machinery made the "good life" possible in America, and examine the impact and evolution of science and technology. Julia Child's kitchen is also here.

Second Floor – Displays on the second floor deal with America as a changing nation. Here you'll find the **Star-Spangled Banner★** that survived British shelling at Fort McHenry in 1814 and inspired America's national anthem.

Star-Spangled Banner

Jeff Tinsley/National Museum of American History

Third Floor – Exhibits here focus on armed-forces history and the development of money. **The American Presidency★** exhibit explores the office of the presidency. The Price of Freedom: Americans at War surveys many of the military conflicts in American history. The third floor now also includes an exhibition "Thanks for the Memories" with highlights from the museum's Music, Sports and Entertainment collections.

National Museum of Natural History★★

Constitution Ave. at 10th St. NW. 202-633-1000. www.mnh. si.edu. Open year-round daily 10am–5:30pm (extended hours Mar–Aug). Closed Dec 25.

From dinosaur bones to glittering gemstones to a creepy-crawly insect zoo, you'll find something for everyone at this Smithsonian facility, which ranks as one of the most visited museums in the world. Two floors of exhibits and two large-format cinemas explore life on earth through clues nature has left behind—among them are Ice Age mammal skeletons and prehistoric fossils as well as artifacts of human cultures past and present. Soon after the completion of the Arts and Industries Building in 1881, more space was needed to accommodate the rapidly expanding collections. In 1903 Congress authorized the construction of the Smithsonian's third building, today known as the National Museum of Natural History. The original four-story granite Classical Revival structure was completed in 1910. Today the expanded 16-acre museum encompasses 300,000 square feet of exhibition space, conserves more than 124 million specimens and provides laboratory facilities for 500 geologists, zoologists, botanists, anthropologists and paleontologists.

National Museum of Natural History, Smithsonian Institution

Tips For Visiting

Start your visit in the first-floor rotunda, dominated by a 13-foot-tall African bush elephant. An information desk to the left of the mall entrance provides a free map and guide. At the rear of the hall is the box office for the IMAX and Immersion theaters. In the Immersion Cinema, audience members can manipulate the onscreen action with their own control panels. Tickets for either theater may be purchased up to two weeks in advance *(call 202-633-4629 or 877-932-4629 for tickets, times and information)*. For a relaxing evening after the exhibits close, head to the museum's Jazz Café, featuring live music on Fridays from 6pm to 10pm *($12)*.

Best of the Natural World

Gem and Mineral Collection★★★ – The museum's most popular attraction is housed in Geology Hall.

Here you'll be dazzled by some of the world's biggest gems (and you thought diamonds were just a girl's best friend!):

- Hope Diamond, the largest blue diamond in the world at 45.5 carats
- Oppenheimer Diamond (uncut and unpolished) at 253.7 carats
- Star of Asia sapphire from Sri Lanka at 330 carats
- Headlight-size golden topaz from Brazil, the largest cut gemstone in the world at 22,892.5 carats
- Hooker Emerald at 75 carats
- Rosser Reeves Ruby at 138.7 carats
- Flawless quartz ball from Burma, measuring 127.88 inches

Dinosaurs and Fossils – Kids love dinosaurs, and the ones at the Natural History Museum put a smile on many a young face. Circling the Dinosaur Hall is a chain of galleries that describe the parade of life from the "Big Bang" 4.6 billion years ago through the Cenozoic era, which continues today. Some of the dino skeletons here include:

- *Triceratops*
- A 90-foot-long *Diplodocus*

Dinasaur Hall

MUSEUMS

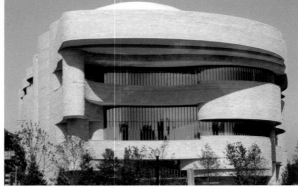
National Museum of the American Indian

Leonda Levchuk/NMAI

- A life-size model of a pterosaur
- *Tyranosaurus rex*
- *Stegosaurus stenops*
- Casts of bone-headed dinosaurs, or pachycephalosaurs

African Voices – This large-scale exhibit uses film clips, recorded narratives, poetry excerpts and music, along with 400 artifacts from the museum's permanent collection, to explore thousands of years of African history.

Discovery Room – Touch and examine various objects and artifacts (fossils, minerals, and animals— both living and preserved).

Insect Zoo – Kids can easily peer into the low cases here, to see living and preserved insects. As a group, arthropods–which make up 90 percent of animal life on earth—have survived for 475 million years. If you're not afraid of spiders, take in one of the tarantula feedings *(Tue–Fri 10:30am, 11:30am & 1:30pm; weekend 11:30am, 12:30pm & 1:30pm)*.

National Museum of the American Indian★★

East end of National Mall at 4th St. and Independence Ave. SW. 202-633-1000. www.american indian.si.edu. Open year-round daily 10am–5:30pm. Closed Dec 25.

The Mall's last open space is now devoted to the first Americans. Opened in September 2004, the NMAI is the first national museum dedicated to Native Americans and the first new museum on the Mall since 1987. Fifteen years in creation, the museum holds 800,000 objects; they represent more than 1,000 indigenous cultures spanning some 10,000 years of North, South, and Central American history.
A curving golden-hued limestone exterior, suggesting a Native American cliff dwelling, stands in contrast to surrounding Classical-style buildings. The 4.25-acre site includes wetlands and 40 boulders, enhancing the museum's emphasis on man as part of the natural world.

Inside, a prism window reflects sunlight into a 120-foot-high atrium, and a wall of video screens welcomes visitors in 150 native languages, indicating the ongoing vitality and diversity of Indian ways. Major exhibits focus on such topics as native cosmologies, history from Indian points of view, and the lifestyles of 21C Indians. The museum's holdings grew from the comprehensive collection of wealthy New York banker **George Gustav Heye** (1874–1957), which he amassed over a 45-year period. Among the treasures are Northwestern wood carvings and masks, Plains Indians clothes and feather bonnets, Southwestern pottery and basketry, Costa Rican ceramics, Mayan jade objects, and Andean gold. Some 8,000 objects are on display at any given time. A **demonstration area** in the atrium offers visitors a chance to see native arts in action; the construction of an Inuit kayak or a Pueblo necklace, for example, gives context to the museum's exhibits.

Native Lunch

The museum's **Mitisam Native Foods Café** continues the aboriginal theme with a taste of Indian cuisines from various regions. Indigenous, and often organic, ingredients are used where possible. Diners can try cedar-planked, fire-roasted salmon; chicken tamales wrapped in corn husks; pinto bean and corn enchiladas; or buffalo burgers and chile fries. For a drink, try the hibiscus flower aqua fresca and for dessert the cinnamon fry bread. Mitisam, by the way, is Piscataway for "let's eat."

National Portrait Gallery★★

Old Patent Office Building, 8th & F Sts. NW. 202-633-8300. www.npg.si.edu. Open year-round daily 10am–5:30pm. Closed Dec 25.

Think of the National Portrait Gallery as America's family album—a huge one that holds 15,000 paintings, sculptures, photographs, engravings and drawings. To be displayed here, portraits must be original works of art and must depict men and women who have made "significant contributions to the history, development and culture" of the US.
The Portrait Gallery occupies the grand **Old Patent Office Building★★**, built in 1867 in the Greek Revival style. It shares this enormous building with the Smithsonian American Art Museum, which it connects to via hallway galleries. If you want a pleasant spot to take a break, head for the interior courtyard, with its cast-iron fountains and monumental sculptures.

First Floor – Here you'll find Champions of American Sport (tennis star Arthur Ashe, baseball's Ty Cobb) and popular figures from the Performing Arts (actress Marilyn Monroe, dancer Martha Graham, composer George Gershwin).

Second Floor – Portraits are arranged in chronological order beginning with the Founding Fathers and leading to the present. Gilbert Stuart's portrait of George Washington that was used for his likeness on the one-dollar bill is here—it's called the **Lansdowne portrait★**. American presidents,

MUSEUMS

Patently New

The historic Old Patent Office Building spans an entire city block in the popular Penn Quarter neighborhoods. After undergoing extensive renovations, the building reopened on July 1, 2006, and was renamed The Donald W. Reynolds Center for American Art and Portraiture. Both the National Portrait Gallery and the Smithsonian American Art Museum are now housed inside.

poets (Carl Sandburg, Robert Frost), Native Americans and giants of industry (J.D. Rockefeller, Andrew Carnegie) are also on view, along with military leaders like Douglas MacArthur and George C. Marshall.

Third Floor – Be sure to see the **Great Hall**, which occupies the south wing. It's decorated with multicolored English tiles, carved ceiling medallions, and a yellow and blue central skylight.

Phillips Collection★★

1600 21st St. NW. 202-387-2151. www.phillipscollection.org. Open year-round Tue–Sat 10am–5pm, Thu 10am–8:30pm, Sun 11am–5pm. Closed Mon & major holidays. $10 weekends (free weekdays).

Are the museums on the Mall overwhelming you? Try this charmer, set on a quiet corner a few short blocks from bustling Dupont Circle.

A small museum of great distinction, the Phillips Collection is the nation's first museum of modern art. Here you'll see outstanding works by prominent American and European artists in an intimate house setting.

The grandson of one of the co-founders of the Jones and Laughlin Steel Co., **Duncan Phillips** (1886–1966) founded this gallery in 1921 in his family's unpretentious brick and brownstone home as a memorial to his father and his brother, James.

Detail of Luncheon of the Boating Party (1880–81) by Pierre-Auguste Renoir

The Phillips Collection

Sunday At The Phillips

If you've got a Sunday afternoon to spare, why not spend it at the Phillips Collection? After you've had your fill of fabulous artwork, you can relax and listen to up-and-coming musical talent from around the world at the Sunday Concert series (free with museum admission). An institution since 1941, Sunday concerts are held from September to May at 5pm in the oak-paneled Music Room. There are no reserved seats, so get there early.

Phillips and his wife, Marjorie Acker, a talented painter in her own right, expanded the collection, which now contains some 2,500 works and includes all the major French Impressionists, post-Impressionists, Cubists and 17C and 18C masters (Goya, El Greco, Chardin).

Phillips Picks

Luncheon of the Boating Party – On exhibit in a second-floor gallery is the museum's most renowned treasure, painted by **Pierre Auguste Renoir** (1841–1919) in 1881. Phillips and his wife purchased this work in 1923, for the record sum of $125,000.

Paul Klee – The second floor contains a room devoted exclusively to the delightful works of the renowned Swiss painter (1879–1940).

Bonnard Collection – Reputed to be the country's largest collection of paintings by French artist **Pierre Bonnard** (1867–1947), this group of works is housed in the adjoining Goh Annex.

Mark Rothko – A small gallery on the first floor displays four important Abstract Expressionist works by Rothko (1903–1970) who is known for his hauntingly simple canvases filled with large expanses of color.

United States Holocaust Memorial Museum★★

South of Independence Ave., between 14th St. & Raoul Wallenberg Pl. SW. 202-488-0400. www.ushmm.org. Open year-round daily 10am–5:30pm. Closed Yom Kippur & Dec 25.

A deeply moving history lesson awaits you at this large museum/research complex, relating the Nazi extermination of six millions Jews and six million others during World War II. Located adjacent to the Bureau of Engraving and Printing, the striking five-story brick and limestone building (1993, I.M. Pei & Partners) is designed as a

Gwen Cannon/Michelin

US Holocaust Museum

MUSEUMS

47

Tips For Visiting

Timed passes, available at the box office, are required for entrance to the permanent exhibit. Advance passes can be obtained from *tickets.com (800-400-9373; service charge applies)*. Instead of viewing the intense permanent exhibit, children can see the special exhibit entitled **Daniel's Story: Remember the Children.**

post-Modern "penitentiary," with "watchtowers" lining the north and south walls. Exposed metal beams and metal-framed glass doors of the Hall of Witness, the building's 7,500-square-foot glass-roofed atrium, amplify the feeling of imprisonment.

Fourth Floor – The compelling permanent exhibit begins on the fourth floor. Before entering the elevator, you'll receive a keepsake photo identification card detailing the background and the fate of a particular Holocaust victim. In darkened surroundings, you're confronted with photographs, films and artifacts. Panels relate the horrific story of the deprivation of property, human rights and eventually the lives of the millions of men, women and children who were systematically murdered.

Third Floor – Concentration-camp life is evoked on the third floor. Personal articles, food bowls and work implements are interspersed with an actual railcar and a scale model of a gas chamber. Especially sensitive topics are presented discreetly, for optional viewing, on sunken video monitors.

Second Floor – Exhibits here hail the valor and success of rescue and resistance efforts. Film footage recording the liberating armies'

arrival at the camps is continually shown. One display focuses on **Raoul Wallenberg**, the Swedish diplomat stationed in Budapest who led the War Refuge Board's mission to save Hungarian Jews. At the end of your visit, you might want to spend some quiet time inside the 60-foot high Hall of Remembrance, an unadorned, light-filled space for contemplation and commemorative ceremonies.

International Spy Museum★

800 F St. NW. at 8th St. 202-393-7798. www.spymuseum.org. Open Apr–Oct 10am–8pm, Nov–Mar 10am–6pm. Closed Jan 1, Thanksgiving Day & Dec 25. $18. Advance tickets recommended.

All is not what it seems. And nowhere is this more true than at the International Spy Museum. If you've ever wondered what it would be like to be a secret agent, here's your chance to adopt a cover identity and learn some of the tricks of this shadowy trade. (They can't give away all the secrets, though—some are classified!). Located across the street from the National Portrait Gallery, the Spy Museum opened in July 2002. This complex of historic 19C buildings houses the world's largest collection of international espionage artifacts on display to the public. Your adventure begins

International Spy Museum

Shoe with heel transmitter (c. 1960s, USSR, KGB issue)

on the third floor, where you'll be assigned a cover identity and confronted with the real world of spying in the **Briefing Film**. Then it's on to the **School for Spies**, to examine gadgets from buttonhole cameras to lipstick pistols and test your skills to see if you're cut out to be a secret agent. Before leaving, check out the museum store, where you can pick up your own disguise or even purchase spy collectibles that were actually used in the field. Want to really channel your inner James Bond? Try the in the hour-long **Operation Spy** during which you can "become" a U.S. intelligence officer trying to locate a missing nuclear device.

Spies Among Us – Discover real-life spy stories from World War II. War of the Spies – See how spy technology developed from Maxwell Smart's shoe phone to sophisticated spy satellites.

21st Century – Face the challenges that the intelligence community deals with today.

Newseum★

555 Pennsylvania Ave. NW. 888-639-7386. www.newseum.org. Open 9am-5pm daily. Closed Thanksgiving, Christmas and New Year's Day. $20.

In today's age of 24-hour news cycles and point-and-click headlines, it seems only fitting that a

---

Eating Undercover

Need to grab a quick bite between missions? Try the **Spy City Café** for fresh sandwiches, soups, pizzas and salads, served cafeteria-style. While you eat, plan your next caper using the tabletop maps of DC spy sites. If you prefer a private place for that secret rendezvous, **Zola** fills the bill. You'll be well concealed here in sleek red velvet booths, which feature spy ovals cut into them so you can make sure you're not being followed. One-way mirrors in the booths let you monitor activity in the kitchen, where the chef whips up acclaimed New American cuisine. Both restaurants are located in the museum complex.

MUSEUMS

The Kreeger Museum
Hidden behind a high wall on 5.5 wooded acres in Georgetown, the Kreeger Museum *(2401 Foxhall Rd. NW, 202-337-3050, www.kreegermuseum.org)* may be visited by guided tour only. Museum highlights include 19C and 20C European paintings as well as African and 20C art. The post-modern mansion was built in the 1960s by David and Carmen Kreeger to house their collection .

museum devoted to the Fourth Estate now occupies 250,000 square-feet of Pennsylvania Avenue between the White House and the Capitol. The Newseum tells the story of news from ancient forms of reporting on cuneiform tablets all the way up to today's world of global digital media.

The impressive building, complete with a 74-foot-high marble engraving of the First Amendment on the facade, houses 14 exhibition galleries and 15 theaters. An immense glass wall on the Pennsylvania Ave side of the steel, stone and glass building, allows passers-by to catch a glimpse of the 90-foot-high atrium and lets visitors appreciate the historic view as they move through the museum's seven levels.

Near the museum's entrance, the front pages of that day's national and international newspapers are enlarged and displayed. The street-level selection is part of the larger **Today's Front Pages** exhibit, which is on the top floor and updated every morning at 6 am. In its original incarnation, the Newseum was over the river in Arlington and was a fraction of its current size. That version closed in 2002 after the Freedom Forum foundation purchased the land on Pennsylvania Ave for $100 million. Six years later on April 11, 2008, the "new" Newseum opened to the public.

Here's some of the who, what, where when, and whys of the inside:

- **Berlin Wall Gallery** – Eight sections of the Berlin Wall stand in the gallery devoted to the

Berlin Wall, Newseum

Photo by Maria Bryk/Newseum

media's role in the wall's history and ultimate fall. The fronts of the 12-foot-high sections that faced West Germany are covered in political graffiti. In stark contrast, the backs, which faced East Germany, were painted white so people attempting to escape could more easily be seen by guards.

- **News Corporation News History Gallery** – A collection of 30,000 historic newspapers serve as the center of this gallery, the museum's largest. Among the highlights are Tim Russert's now famous dry-erase board from the 2000 presidential election and the November 3, 1948, edition of the Chicago Daily Tribune which proclaims, "Dewey Defeats Truman."

- **Comcast 9/11 Gallery** – The September 11th exhibit was mounted not as a memorial but as a way to show how journalists in New York, Pennsylvania and at the Pentagon reported the deadly attacks. Front pages from newspapers from all 50 states, DC, and 34 countries are displayed on the gallery's north wall.
A mangled piece of the antenna mast from the World Trade Center's North Tower is also here. A short film with first-person accounts from journalists who covered the attacks plays in the theater behind the north wall. Discreetly placed tissue canisters can be found on the way out of the theater.

National Museum of Women in the Arts★

1250 New York Ave. at 13th St. NW. 202-783-5000. www.nmwa.org. Open year-round Mon–Sat 10am–5pm, Sun noon–5pm. Closed Jan 1, Thanksgiving Day & Dec 25. $10.

Everything here is woman-made. Behind this Beaux-Arts exterior is the world's only major museum devoted exclusively to the works of women artists. Devoting itself to recognizing the achievements of women artists of all periods and nationalities, the National Museum of Women in the Arts maintains a 3,000-piece permanent collection that spans the years from the 16C to the present and covers every medium from native American pottery to abstract sculpture. Local philanthropists Wilhelmina and Wallace Holladay founded the museum in 1981 as a private institution "to encourage greater awareness of women in the arts and their contributions to the history of art." The Holladays donated their own collection to form the core of the museum's holdings,

Courtesy of National Museum of Women in the Arts, Gift of Wallace and Wilhelmina Holladay

Lady with a Bowl of Violets (c.1910) by Lilla Cabot Perry

MUSEUMS

which today comprises works by more than 800 women artists.

In 1983 the museum purchased its present building from the fraternal order of Masons and transformed the interior into three levels of exhibit space, a library and research center, and a 200-seat auditorium, where public lectures, films and concerts are held. Works from the permanent collection are displayed in the two-story marble **Great Hall** and on the mezzanine; the second and third floors are reserved for temporary exhibits.

A Sampling of Superlatives

Oldest Work – The museum's oldest painting is Portrait of a Noblewoman (c. 1580) by Lavinia Fontana, a 16C Italian painter from Bologna who is considered the first professional woman artist.

19C Sculpture – A rare medium for female artists of that period, 19C sculpture includes pieces by Camille Claudel, Malvina Hoffman and Bessie Potter Vonnoh.

20C Paintings – Alligator Pears in a Basket (1921) by Georgia O'Keeffe; Self-Portrait Dedicated to Leon Trotsky (1937) by Mexican artist Frida Kahlo; Singing Their Songs (1992) by African-American painter Elizabeth Catlett.

Renwick Gallery ★

Pennsylvania Ave. & 17th St. NW. 202-633-2850. www.americanart. si.edu. Open year-round daily 10am–5:30pm. Closed Dec 25.

If your only exposure to American arts and crafts has been at seasonal local craft fairs, you'll be surprised at the high quality of contemporary and traditional American craftsmanship displayed here. From striking contemporary quilts to delicate art glass to fanci-ful hand-wrought iron gates, the variety of the Renwick's collection will amaze you.

Located just across the street from the White House, the Second Empire-style gem is named for its architect, William Renwick Jr. (whose claims to fame include the Smithsonian Castle and Saint Patrick's Cathedral in New York City). This was the original home of the **Corcoran Gallery** *(see p34),* commissioned in 1858 by financier William Wilson Corcoran. With its distinctive mansard roof, the lovely redbrick building is decorated with square sandstone columns and garlands. The Renwick's permanent collection is displayed on the second floor. Here you'll see outstanding 20C crafts, rang-

---

Jackie Saves The Day

In 1874 the Corcoran Gallery of Art, as the building was then called, opened as Washington's first art museum. By 1897, the collection had grown too large for its original digs and William Corcoran built the present-day Corcoran Museum to house his treasures. Sold to the government for $300,000, the old building was used by the US Court of Claims until 1964, when demolition was pro-posed. Former First Lady Jacqueline Kennedy led the campaign to preserve the landmark, and in 1965 President Lyndon Johnson turned the building over to the Smithsonian as a gallery of "art, crafts and design." Restored to its original appearance, the refurbished Renwick opened as a department of the Smithso-nian American Art Museum in 1972.

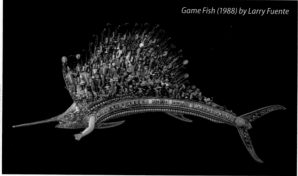

Game Fish (1988) by Larry Fuente

Smithsonian American Art Museum

ing from traditional basketry to abstract works in glass, wood, clay, metal and fiber. First-floor galleries focus on temporary exhibits.

Smithsonian American Art Museum★

Old Patent Office Building, 8th & G Sts. NW. Entrance on G St. 202-633-1000. http://americanart. si.edu. Open daily 11:30 am–7 pm. Closed Dec 25.

Sure, Europe claims more than its share of fine art, but don't overlook the US. The Smithsonian American Art Museum is the country's only museum dedicated to art and artists of the United States. Containing nearly 40,000 works by 7,000 American artists, the permanent collection spans 300 years, from Colonial quilts to American Impressionist paintings to 21C art glass.

Located in the landmark Old Patent Office Building, this museum contains the country's oldest federal collection of art, which began when Washingtonian John Varden donated his collection of artwork to the federal government in 1841. In 1862 that collection was transferred to the Smithsonian Institution, and eventually ended up in the Old Patent Office Building. Named the National Museum of American Art (NMAA) in 1980, the facility was renamed the Smithsonian American Art Museum in 2000 to better reflect its mission of displaying exclusively the works of US artists. The renovation, which was completed in 2006, added a new roof and additional gallery space, among other features.

Touring Exhibits
African-American Masters – Some 61 works here, by the likes of Richmond Barthé, Romare Bearden and William H. Johnson, incorporate social influences such as politics, spirituality, music and folkore.

The Land Through A Lens – Photographs by Ansel Adams, Timothy O'Sullivan, Aaron Siskind and others capture the beauty and symbolism of America's land.

Graphic Masters – Works on paper from the 1860s to the 1990s spotlight watercolors, drawings and pastels by a host of American artists.

MUSEUMS

Masters of Their Craft –
This exhibit showcases pieces in clay, fiber, glass, metal and wood, including glass sculptures by Dale Chihuly.

Calico and Chintz – The 22 extraordinary quilts in this display were hand-crafted in America before 1850.

Stephen F. Udvar-Hazy Center★

South of Dulles International Airport, VA, at the intersection of Rtes. 28 and 50, in Chantilly, VA. 202-633-1000. www.nasm.si.edu/museum/udvarhazy. Open year-round daily 10am–5:30pm. Closed Dec 25. Parking $12. A shuttle (fee) runs between the Center and the National Air and Space Museum on the Mall downtown.

If the spacious halls of the National Air and Space Museum only leave you asking for more, there is now a fine sequel. Designed to coincide with the centennial of the Wright Brothers' first manned, powered flight, NASM's newest facility opened on 175 acres adjacent to Dulles Airport in December 2003. The Udvar-Hazy Center, named for

Who is Udvar-Hazy?
Chairman and CEO of International-al Lease Finance Corporation, the top commercial aircraft owner/lessor, Steven F. Udvar-Hazy do-nated $65 million toward the $311 million museum cost, one of the largest gifts to the Smithsoni-an from an individual. Udvar-Hazy emigrated to the United States from Hungary as a boy; he has an FAA Airline Transport Pilot license and has logged over 6,000 hours of flying time.

its major benefactor, displays more than 200 aircraft and spacecraft in its 10-story-high, 986-foot-long **Aviation Hangar**. Inside, visitors have access to elevated walkways from which they can view aircraft displayed on the floor and sus-pended from above.

Aircraft – One of the highlights on display is the "Enola Gay," the Boeing B-29 Superfortress from which an atomic bomb was dropped on Hiroshima, Japan on August 6, 1945; commander Col. Paul W. Tibbets, Jr. named the plane for his mother. The "Enola Gay" is on display after a 10-year restoration.

Aviation Hanger, Steven F. Udvar-Hazy Center

Cynthia Ochterbeck/Michelin

MUST SEE

McDonnell Space Hangar – Large artifacts here include an AGM-86B cruise missile, two Mercury space capsules, and a Redstone Missile rocket engine. The museum also harbors more than 1,500 display artifacts, including models, aircraft machine guns, spacesuits, and satellites. A 164-foot-high **observation tower** provides a great viewpoint for visitors to watch planes land and take off from Dulles, and a 479-seat IMAX theater offers yet another large window onto the aviation world.

National Building Museum

401 F. St. NW, between 4th & 5th Sts. 202-272-2448. www.nbm.org. Open year-round Mon–Sat 10am– 5pm, Sun 11am–5pm. Closed Jan 1, Thanksgiving Day & Dec 25.

Here's a building devoted to buildings. Yes, you read that right. The National Building Museum celebrates America's achievement in the building arts. Housed in the 1887 **Pension Building★**, the museum's exhibits demystify the building process and show changing architectural styles and construction techniques.

To this end, the permanent collection claims 40,000 photographs, 68,000 prints and drawings, and 2,100 objects, including architectural elements and samples of building materials.

Exhibits, which change frequently, are arranged around a vast interior court known as the **Great Hall.** Measuring 316 feet long, the Great Hall is lined with eight 75-foot Corinthian columns painted to look like marble.

Building Family

Plan on taking some young construction workers to the National Building Museum?

If so, make sure to "check out" one of the museum's Family Tool Kits ($5 per kit). These activity sets, designed to be used together by adults and children, provide fun activities to help keep little hands happy and busy. There are three different tool kits for rent: Patterns (for ages 3-7), Eye Spy (for ages 7-10), and Construction Detector (for ages 8-11).

National Building Museum

Gwen Cannon/Michelin

MEMORIALS

The section of the Mall west of 15th Street is the setting for the nation's most revered monuments. Roughly ringing the Tidal Basin—whose banks are famous for the flowering Japanese cherry trees that burst with pink blossoms in early spring—the memorials here and around the city honor some of the greatest and most heroic Americans.

Franklin Delano Roosevelt Memorial ★★★

Tidal Basin, west of the Jefferson Memorial. 202-619-7222 or 202-426-6843. www.nps.gov/frde. Open year-round 24 hours daily. Interpretive ranger station open 9:30am–11:30pm daily. (closed Dec 25.)

Franklin Delano Roosevelt Memorial

Destination DC

Set along the famous **Cherry Tree Walk** bordering the Tidal Basin, this memorial to the nation's 32nd president brings to life the four

Monuments by Night

After dark and the crowds have departed, the monuments are lit up and become even more beautiful. Ask at the visitor center *(see Practical Information)* about guided tours by bus or bike. If you have your own car then for a special and unique experience park up and walk to see the FDR memorial under the stars.

terms of office held by Franklin D. Roosevelt. Ornamental plantings, waterfalls and quiet pools create a feeling of tranquility at the expansive memorial, which opened in May 1997.

Born to wealthy parents in New York, Franklin Roosevelt (1882–1945) graduated from Harvard University and Columbia University Law School. He entered politics in 1910 when he was elected to the New York Senate.

As US president, FDR led the nation through some of the most difficult periods in its history—the Great Depression and World War II. Through his radio "fireside chats,"

A Courageous Spirit

In January 2001 President Bill Clinton dedicated an addition to the FDR memorial. Located at the site's entrance, a bronze statue sculpted by Robert Graham depicts FDR sitting in the wheelchair he used daily after polio crippled him in 1921. Although the idea of illustrating FDR in his wheelchair met with great controversy, officials eventually decided that the statue emphasized Roosevelt's indomitable spirit.

A Man For All Seasons

Thomas Jefferson (1743–1826) was a true Renaissance man. In addition to being a skilled statesman, Jefferson was equally celebrated as an architect, philosopher, horticulturist, musician and inventor. In 1774 the native Virginian was elected to the first Continental Congress in Philadelphia. At the second Continental Congress a year later, he was appointed to a committee charged with drafting a statement to the British Crown that justified the colonists' stand on independence. Noted for his eloquent writings, Jefferson was encouraged to draft the document himself. On July 4, 1776, the **Declaration of Independence** was signed by the Continental Congress.

Roosevelt inspired optimism and courage in the American people. Four outdoor galleries of red South Dakota granite symbolize each of FDR's terms as president:

First-Term Room (1933–37) focuses on the president's determination to overcome the nation's economic problems.

Second-Term Room (1937–41) represents the US in the depths of the Great Depression.

Third-Term Room (1941–45) uses a jumbled landscape of jagged granite blocks to symbolize the devastation of World War II.

Fourth-Term Room (1945) depicts the president's death. A statue of Eleanor Roosevelt commemorates her role as First Lady and first delegate to the United Nations.

Jefferson Memorial★★★

Ohio Dr., on the south bank of the Tidal Basin. 202-246-6821. www. nps.gov/thje. Open year-round daily. Ranger station open 9:30am to 11:30pm daily. (Closed Dec 25.)

You might think that the south bank of the Tidal Basin is a strange place for the Roman Pantheon. No, your eyes aren't playing tricks on you—this is a 20C adaptation, designed by John Russell Pope in 1936 to pay homage to the

Destination DC

Jefferson Memorial

MEMORIALS

nation's third president, Thomas Jefferson (1801–1809).

Opened to the public in 1942, the white marble monument echoes the Classical style of architecture that Jefferson reproduced at Monticello, his Virginia home *(see Excursions)*. Visitors enter through a columned entrance portico that rises from a wide paved plaza. Before you go in, look up to the front of the pediment, where sculpted images show Jefferson surrounded by the four other members of the committee chosen to draft the Declaration of Independence: Benjamin Franklin, John Adams, Roger Sherman and Robert Livingston.

Inside the memorial's open-air interior stands an imposing 19-foot-tall bronze statue of a middle-aged Thomas Jefferson, by sculptor Rudolph Evans. Jefferson's likeness clutches a rolled parchment on which the Declaration of Independence is written.

Korean War Memorial

©Rimas Zilinskas/Dreamstime.com

"The Forgotten War"

American veterans of the Korean War (1950–1953) attached this nickname to a war they felt was overshadowed by World War II and the controversy of Vietnam.

As memories of Korea faded from the national consciousness, veterans pursued a means to formally commemorate the war.

In 1986 Congress authorized a commission to oversee the design of a memorial. The memorial was dedicated in 1995 by President Bill Clinton and Kim Young Sam, president of the Republic of Korea, on the 42nd anniversary of the war's armistice.

Korean War Veterans Memorial★★★

Independence Ave. at French Dr. SW. 202-426-6841. www.nps. gov/kowa. Open year-round daily. Rangers on duty from 9:30am to 11:30pm daily. Closed Dec 25.

The first thing you see as you approach the Korean War Veterans Memorial is a "field" dotted with 19 larger-than-life stainless-steel statues (each about 7 feet tall) of men in patrol formation wearing combat rain gear. One side of the field is lined with a 164-foot-long wall of polished black granite, sandblasted with the faces of more than 2,500 servicemen and women. Although they are not identified, these faces were taken from actual photographs of people who participated in the Korean conflict. Mounted in the granite, an American flag waves over the inscription: "Our nation honors her sons and daughters who answered the call to defend a country they never knew and a people they never met."

The rim of the circular **Pool of Remembrance**, located behind the flagpole, is etched with the statistics of the lives that were sacrificed in this conflict. Of the 1.5 million Americans who served in the Korean War, more than 54,000 died, some 110,000 were captured or wounded and 8,000 were declared missing.

Lincoln Memorial★★★

The Mall at 23rd St. NW. 202-426-6841. www.nps.gov/linc. Open year-round daily. Rangers on duty 8am–11:45pm. Closed Dec 25.

Reproduced on the copper penny and the $5 bill, the facade of the Lincoln Memorial is easy to identify. Architect Henry Bacon designed his version of a Greek temple as a tribute to the nation's 16th president (1861–65). Thirty-six Doric columns—symbolizing the 36 states in the Union at the time of Lincoln's death—form a continuous ring around the monument (states' names are inscribed above the columns). In 1922 the Lincoln Memorial was dedicated in a ceremony attended by Robert Todd Lincoln, the presi-

Statue of Abraham Lincoln, Lincoln Memorial

©James Boulette/iStockphoto.com

dent's only surviving son.
From its stately perch atop a long flight of stairs, the famous marble image of a seated, brooding Lincoln stares out across the city. Renowned 19C sculptor Daniel Chester French created this powerful, 175 ton, 19-foot-high marble **statue★★★** that captures Lincoln's strength. The left wall of the memorial is inscribed with Lincoln's celebrated Gettysburg Address (1863). Stop at the top of the memorial's steps to take in the grand **view★★** of the Mall from the **Reflecting Pool**, which stretches 350 feet beyond the Lincoln Memorial, to the Washington

Honest Abe

Abraham Lincoln (1809–1865), The down-home statesman known as "Honest Abe", is remembered as the Great Emancipator who freed the country from the shackles of slavery. A month after his 1861 inauguration, the first shots of the Civil War were fired at Fort Sumter. In 1863 Lincoln issued the Emancipation Proclamation. The proclamation set the stage for the passage of the 13th Amendment to the Constitution in 1865, which finally abolished slavery.

In April 1865, at the start of Lincoln's second term, the long war ended. On April 14, 1865, Lincoln was shot at Ford's Theatre by actor John Wilkes Booth *(see Historic Sites/Ford's Theatre)*. The following day, at age 56, President Abraham Lincoln died of his wounds.

Enough Already?
With the Mall sprouting monuments as frequently as protesters, many people have tried to halt Mall sprawl. Though some 450 veterans organizations supported the World War II Memorial, a vocal opposition worried about the potential loss of sweeping views. Mall conservationists may be fighting a losing battle—plans in the works for memorials on or near the Mall include ones honoring Martin Luther King, Jr., Black Patriots of the American Revolution, and John Adams and his family.

Monument. In 1963, these same steps were the setting for Martin Luther King's legendary 'I Have a Dream' speech.

National World War II Memorial★★★

National Mall at 17th St. between Constitution & Independence Aves. 202-619-7222. www.nps. gov/nwwm. Open 24 hours daily. Ranger station open 9:30am to 11:30pm daily. (Closed Dec 25.)

The latest memorial to grace the Mall, the World War II Memorial opened in April 2004. Situated between the Lincoln Memorial and the Washington Monument, the memorial pays tribute to the 16 million United States citizens who served in the armed forces during the greatest conflict of the 20th century. The memorial also honors the Americans who died and the spirit, sacrifice and commitment of the American people during that time. Providing a parklike serenity, about two-thirds of the memorial's 7.4 acres are composed of landscaping and water elements.

Memorial Plaza – One of two central design features (along with the Rainbow Pool), the granite and bronze plaza features an entrance inlaid with seals of the Army, Navy, Marine Corps, Army Air Forces, Coast Guard, and Merchant Marine. A series of 24 bronze bas reliefs on balustrades depict America during the war. Pavilions, one on each end of the plaza, display four bronze columns topped by bronze eagles clutching victory laurels. Curving ramps then

National World War II Memorial

Gwen Cannon/Michelin

lead onto the 338-foot-long plaza. The plaza's Freedom Wall supports 4,000 gold stars, commemorating the 400,000 Americans who gave their lives.

Rainbow Pool – Lined with granite benches for peaceful reflection, the 247-foot-long pool, complete with fountains, spreads across the middle of the Mall, thus leaving open views to other Mall monuments. Spaced about the pool stand 56 17-foot-tall granite pillars, celebrating the nation's unity during World War II—each state, territory, and the District of Columbia are represented.

Vietnam Veterans Memorial

Gwen Cannon/Michelin

Vietnam Veterans Memorial★★★

Bacon Dr. & Constitution Ave. NW. 202-619-7222 or 202-426-6841. www.nps.gov/vive. Open year-round daily Ranger station open 9:30 am to 11:30pm. Closed Dec 25. Directories specifying the memorial panels on which names appear are located at the approaches to the Wall.

Known simply as "the Wall," the Vietnam Veterans Memorial is tucked away in the sylvan setting of Constitution Gardens. Though it was conceived in controversy, this solemn black-granite wall has become one of America's most cherished and moving shrines—a place of healing where family and friends can touch the names of loved ones lost in battle.

Inset in a low hill, the 493.5-foot-long memorial is actually made up of two triangular panels that join at a 125-degree angle. The two arms of the wall point toward the Washington Monument and the Lincoln Memorial. Their polished surfaces are inscribed with the names of 58,226 men and women killed or missing in the Vietnam War. Beginning with the

"Serenity, Without Conflict"

The idea for this monument came from a small group of Vietnam veterans living in the capital. Troubled by the public's indifference toward those Americans who served in the Southeast Asian conflict, they formed the Vietnam Veterans Memorial Fund in 1979 to solicit congressional support and to set up fundraising efforts. In 1980, President Jimmy Carter signed a resolution authorizing the creation of the monument. The Wall was dedicated in November 1982.

The national design competition for the memorial attracted 1,421 entries. The winning design was submitted by Maya Ying Lin, a 21-year-old architectural student at Yale University. Lin's wall was conceived as a symbol of healing. As she explained, "Take a knife and cut open the earth, and with time the grass would heal it."

first casualty in 1959 and ending in 1975, the names are arranged chronologically, according to when each died or was declared missing in action. Those who died in the war have diamonds next to their names; those missing or imprisoned are indicated by a cross.

Vietnam Women's Memorial – In a grove of trees just south of the Wall stands a bronze statue (1992, Glenna Goodacre) of three military women tending a wounded soldier; this memorial is dedicated to the more than 265,000 women who served in Vietnam.

The Washington Monument★★★

On the Mall at 15th St. Timed admission tickets are required. Free same-day tickets are available from the kiosk at 15th St. & Madison Dr. 202-233-3520. www.nps.gov/wamo. Open year-round daily 9am–5pm (extended summer hours). Advance reservations ($1.50 fee) can be made by calling 877-444-6777 or online at www.recreation.gov. Closed Dec 25 and July 4.

This 555-foot-tall white marble obelisk is hard to miss. It's the

Washington Monument

©S. Greg Panosian/iStockphoto.com

Washington Monument Statistics

Height: 555ft 5⅛in
Weight: 90,854 tons
Thickness at base: 15ft
Thickness at top: 18in
Width at base: 55ft 1½ in
Width at top: 34ft 5½ in
Depth of foundation: 36ft 10in
Cost: $1,187,710.00

capital's most conspicuous landmark as well as the world's tallest freestanding stone structure. A tribute to America's first president, George Washington (1789–97), the Washington Monument is also an icon of the city that bears his name. Prominent architect Robert Mills designed the shaft, whose

Just George

George Washington (1732–1799) began his long military service in his early twenties as a commander during the French and Indian War. A member of the Virginia House of Burgesses, Washington became increasingly disenchanted with Britain as resentment over British taxation grew among the colonists. In 1774 he served as a delegate to the Continental Congress. A year later, Washington was unanimously elected the Continental Army's commander. In 1787, when lack of centralized government threatened the new confederation of states, he presided over the Constitutional Congress in Philadelphia. Two years later, the new electoral college unanimously voted Washington the first president of the new nation. After two terms, he refused a third.

cornerstone was laid on July 4, 1848. Construction proceeded slowly, with ever-insufficient funds finally running dry in 1853. The unfinished obelisk sat neglected until President Ulysses S. Grant authorized its completion 25 years later. In 1888 the Washington Monument officially opened. Take the elevator up to the top, where small windows afford some of the best panoramic **views★★★** of the city.

Pentagon Memorial

On the Pentagon grounds in Arlington, Virginia. http://memorial.pentagon.mil. 703-545-6700 or 703-428-0711. Open 24 hours a day year round.

As the world watched the devastating events of September 11, 2001, unfold on television, Washingtonians watched them happen in their backyard. Residents of the city looked on in horror as the billows of smoke rose up from the banks of the Potomac River as they scrambled to find safety and connect with loved ones. Tragically, some never did. On that infamous day American Airlines Flight 77 was taken hostage and flown into the Pentagon. Along with those killed in New York and Pennsylvania, 125 people in the Pentagon and all 59 people aboard Flight 77 lost their lives. Soon after the attack, Congress authorized the creation of a permanent memorial to the victims on the grounds of the Pentagon. Seven years later on September 11, 2008, the Pentagon Memorial became a reality when it was officially dedicated to an audience made up of dignitaries and the family and friends of the victims. The memorial opened to

the public on September 12, 2008. The Pentagon Memorial embraces a simple yet powerful design that honors the dead while providing a reflective space for visitors. Built on 1.9 acres of land next to the Pentagon, the memorial stands within view of the spot where the plane crashed into the building. The memorial's centerpiece is 184 cantilevered benches; one for every victim. The names of the victims are inscribed on each bench. The benches are set up as a timeline showing the ages of those who died—the first one is for three-year-old Dana Falkenberg and the final one is for John D. Yamnicky, 71. A rectangular reflective pool sits beneath the bench and maple trees have been planted throughout the memorial park. Each memorial is positioned in order to distinguish victims on board Flight 77 from victims within the Pentagon. When visitors read the names of those who were on American Airlines Flight 77 they will face the sky. When standing at a memorial unit dedicated to a victim who was inside the Pentagon, the visitor sees the victim's name and the Pentagon in the same view. The Pentagon Memorial's powerful design came from the creative minds of architects Keith Kaseman and Julie Beckman (Kaseman Beckman Advanced Strategies). The pair were selected as the winners of the international competition held in 2002 to design the new memorial. More than a thousand design teams submitted proposals. A committee of family members of those who died in the attack has been involved with every phase of the project.

HISTORIC SITES

These venerable landmarks are a testament to the eminent men and women of Washington who continually strove to better their city.

Dumbarton Oaks★★

1703 32nd St. NW. 202-339-6400. www.doaks.org. Museum open year-round Tue–Sun 2pm–5pm. Closed Mon & major holidays. Gardens closed in bad weather. Gardens open mid-Mar–Oct daily 2pm–6pm. Rest of the year daily 2pm–5pm. $8, $5 children and senior citizens. Group tours are offered of the garden and collections, free lecture series and music series.

If you think Dumbarton Oaks is just another house museum, you're in for a surprise. Inside this early-19C residence, you'll discover a fabulous collection of Byzantine and pre-Columbian art. In 1920 Robert and Mildred Bliss purchased the estate, restored it to the Federal style and hired renowned landscape gardener Beatrix Farrand to design extensive gardens. Although Robert Bliss' career in the foreign service prevented the couple from living here until 1933, while they were abroad the

Blisses began collecting Byzantine artifacts. When they returned, they added two pavilions and an enclosed courtyard to display their collection to the public. In 1940 the Blisses gave the house, gardens and their Byzantine collection to Harvard University, which still maintains the estate as a research institution and museum. In 1959, the Blisses commissioned Philip Johnson to design a space for the pre-Columbian objects and Frederic Rheinlander King of the architectural firm of Wyeth & King to create the Garden Library Rare Book Room for Mildred Bliss's collection of rare books and manuscripts on garden design, botanical illustration, and horticulture.

Byzantine Collection★★ – More than 1,500 artifacts represent the Byzantine period (4C–15C). These items range from 11C illuminated manuscripts to the collection of 12,000 Byzantine coins, one of the most extensive in the world.

Byzantine Collection, Dumbarton Oaks

Dumbarton Oaks

Conversations Of Consequence

With its 16C stone chimney piece and antique European furnishings, the lovely **Music Room★** was added to the house in 1929. Tapestries and priceless paintings, including The Visitation (c. 1610) by El Greco, decorate the walls. In 1938 Russian composer Igor Stravinsky was commissioned to create a chamber work which was conducted by Nadia Boulanger here. But the room is perhaps most noteworthy for hosting delegates from the US, the Soviet Union, China, and the United Kingdom in 1944. These meetings, now known as the "Dumbarton Oaks Conversations," helped lay the groundwork for the founding of the U.N.

Pre-Columbian Collection★ – Formerly housed in the National Gallery of Art and since 1963 in the Johnson addition, the Blisses' remarkable collection of objects from Mexico, Central American and South America date back as far as Mexico's Olmec culture (1200 BC).

Gardens★★ – *Entrance at 31st & R Sts. NW.* Ten acres of formal gardens designed by Beatrix Farrand surround Dumbarton Oaks. Added in the 1960s, the graceful **Pebble Garden** is a shallow pool framed by curving borders of velvety moss. The bed of the pool is paved with a mosaic of Mexican stones and 19th century orangery.

Washington National Cathedral★★

Massachusetts & Wisconsin Aves, NW. 202-537-6200. www.national cathedral.org. Open Mon–Fri 10am–5:30pm, Sat 10am–4:30pm, Sun 8am–6:30pm. Tue and Thu in the summer until 8pm.

Washington, DC is proud to claim the second-largest cathedral in the US (St. John the Divine in New York City is the largest) and the sixth-largest cathedral in the world. Officially named the Cathedral Church of Saint Peter and Saint Paul, the Gothic-style National Cathedral (as it's more popularly known) overlooks the city from its 57-acre perch atop Mount St. Alban.

The inspiration for a national cathedral dates back to Pierre L'Enfant's grand plan for the capital. Although L'Enfant proposed "a great church for national purposes," the idea won little support at first, since the new nation was committed to the separation of church and state. Finally in 1893 Congress authorized the charter of the Protestant Episcopal Cathedral Foundation. Under the leadership

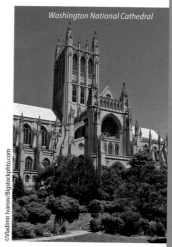

Washington National Cathedral

©Vladimir Ivanov/Bigstockphto.com

Can You Find Darth Vader?
Before the National Cathedral was completed, a contest was held to challenge children to design a sculpture to decorate the exterior of the building. The third-place winner proposed a statue of *Star Wars* villain Darth Vader. If you look with binoculars, you'll see Darth's head high up on the northwest tower.

of the Right Reverend Dr. Yates Satterlee, first Episcopal bishop of Washington, the foundation purchased the Mount St. Alban site at the turn of the 19C. Bishop Satterlee envisioned a Gothic cathedral that would welcome all, regardless of faith or nationality. In a ceremony held on September 29, 1990—exactly 83 years to the day after the foundation was laid—the final stone was set in place on the St. Paul Tower (south side of the main facade).

Cool Facts About the Cathedral

- Designed to carry rainwater away from the walls, 110 gargoyles and grotesques decorate the flying buttresses that support the vaulting of the nave.
- The cathedral's nave is 10 stories high and approximately 565 feet long.

- The centerpiece of the Indiana limestone facade is the 26-foot **rose window**—an abstract composition of 10,500 pieces of colored glass by stained-glass artist Rowan LeCompte.
- Reverend Dr. Martin Luther King Jr. delivered his last Sunday sermon here on March 31, 1968.
- Among the notable Americans interred in the vast underground **crypt** are Helen Keller, her teacher Anne Sullivan, and President Woodrow Wilson.

Decatur House★

1610 H St. NW. 202-842-0920. www.decaturhouse.org. Open year-round Tue–Sat 10am–5pm, Sun noon–4pm. Closed most holidays.

You'd never guess by looking at this sedate 1818 brick town house that the residence saw some pretty lavish parties in its day.

Decatur House

©Richard Gunion/Dreamstime.com

The first home built on Lafayette Square—then called President's Park—across from the White House, Decatur House was built for 19C naval hero **Stephen Decatur**. Today eight first-floor rooms, decorated to reflect the period when the Decaturs lived here, show off the museum's collection of 19C silver, textiles, ceramics, furniture and paintings. Decatur's acts of heroism against the British in the War of 1812 earned him the rank of Captain and a substantial monetary prize. (In those days, the US Navy awarded cash prizes to men who captured enemy vessels.) With his newfound wealth, he commissioned eminent architect Benjamin H. Latrobe to design a home "fit for entertaining." The three-story structure cost Decatur $11,000. He and his wife, Susan, threw big parties here for DC politicos, but only for a brief 14 months. At the age of 41, the young commodore was killed in a duel with a discredited naval officer who held Decatur responsible for his disgrace. Bereft, Mrs. Decatur moved to a Georgetown town house and rented the Lafayette Square house to a succession of dignitaries. The property's Gadsby Wing houses one of the few remaining examples of slave quarters in urban areas and is the only lasting physical evidence that African-Americans were held in bondage in sight of the White House.

A Houseful of Statesmen and Socialites

- Secretary of State Henry Clay lived here in the 1820s, calling it "the best private dwelling in the City."
- After Clay, Martin Van Buren, then secretary of State and soon to be president, occupied the house.
- In 1836 hotelier John Gadsby purchased the residence from Mrs. Decatur.
- Edward Fitzgerald Beale, a renowned Western adventurer, became owner of the house after the Civil War. For two decades Beale and his wife, Mary, were prominent members of the capital's social circles.

Folger Shakespeare Library★

[M] refers to map on inside front cover. 201 E. Capitol St. SE, between 2nd & 3rd Sts. 202-544-7077. www.folger.edu. Open year-round Mon–Sat 10am–5pm. Closed Sun & federal holidays. Free docent-led tours daily.

Much ado about nothing? Quite the contrary. The Folger Library contains the world's largest collection of Shakespeare's printed

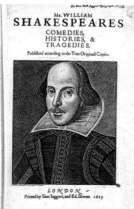

Folger Shakespeare Library

Title page of 1623 First Folio

MUST SEE

The Bard's Birthday Party

Each April the Folger celebrates Shakespeare's birthday (www.folger.edu/birthday) with a free program of Renaissance entertainment, and spontaneous performances of the Bard's work. This is the one day of the year when the Folger's Reading Rooms are open to the public. The kids can have their fortune told, write with quill pens, and participate in other Elizabethan crafts and games. Plus, birthday cake for everyone! As he would say, "All's well that ends well."

works as well as rare Renaissance books and manuscripts. **Henry Clay Folger** (1857–1930) first became interested in Shakespeare while he was at Amherst College, where he went to hear a lecture on Shakespeare by Ralph Waldo Emerson. In 1889 Folger purchased his first rare book of Shakespeare's plays at auction, for a little over $100. He was hooked. The future chairman of the board of New York's Standard Oil Company and his wife, Emily, devoted themselves to gathering books, manuscripts, paintings and other objects relating to the Bard. In the early 1900s, the Folgers decided that their collection needed a permanent home where the public could access it. Although they considered both Stratford-Upon-Avon (Shakespeare's hometown in England) and New York City as locations for their library, they finally settled on the nation's capital. Shortly after the cornerstone for the new Art Deco building was laid in 1930, Henry Folger died unexpectedly following minor surgery. His library, which opened in 1932, is now administered by the trustees of Amherst College in Massachusetts.

Great Hall – In this 190-foot-long room with its barrel-vaulted ceiling, the Library mounts two

to three major exhibitions a year focused on Shakespeare or his era.

Folger Elizabethan Theatre – Inspired by the design of Elizabethan performance spaces, this 250-seat theater is the setting for Folger Theatre productions, poetry readings, lectures, and concerts.

Ford's Theatre and Petersen House★

10th St. NW, between E & F Sts. 202-426-6924. www.nps.gov/foth. Open year-round daily 9am–5pm. Closed Dec 25 & during rehearsals & performances. Timed entry; $1.50 to secure advanced tickets (limited number of free, same-day tickets held at box office each day.)

Going to see a play isn't normally a dangerous form of entertainment. But President Abraham Lincoln's night out at Ford's Theatre in 1865 turned out to be not just dangerous, but fatal. On the evening of April 14, 1865, just five days after General Robert E. Lee had surrendered to Union commander Ulysses S. Grant at Appomattox, Virginia, President and Mrs. Lincoln attended a performance of Our American Cousin at Ford's Theatre. The Lincolns were engrossed in the third act when John Wilkes Booth silently entered the box and shot the president at close range. Booth leaped over the balustrade

Ford's Theatre

©Jason Maehl/Bigstockphoto.com

and escaped on a horse that he had waiting for him in the alley. The wounded president was carried across the street to a boarding house owned by a tailor named Petersen. As the night passed, Cabinet ministers, physicians and others gathered in the back parlor, while friends consoled Mrs. Lincoln in the front parlor. Lincoln never regained consciousness; he died there at 7:22am the following morning.

Ford's Theatre

When John Ford opened the doors of this brick structure in 1863, it was one of the grandest theaters in the country, with a seating capacity of 1,500. After Lincoln's assassination, the federal government closed the theater. Ford's announced intention to continue dramatic productions in the theater met with threats, so the War Department ultimately purchased the building from Ford and began converting it into office space. In the mid-1960s Congress authorized a restoration of the playhouse to its 1865 appearance. Ford's Theatre reopened in

1968 eight years later as both a memorial to Lincoln and an active playhouse *(see Performing Arts)*. The box where Lincoln sat is decorated as it was on the night of April 14, 1865, with the settee that had been specially placed there for the presidential party.

On that fateful night President Lincoln was actually sitting in a rocking chair currently housed at the Ford Museum in Dearborn, Michigan. In the basement, the refurbished **Lincoln Museum** (same hours as the theater) displays such artifacts as Booth's gun and the clothes Lincoln was wearing when he was shot. It also explores Lincoln's life in Washington.

Petersen House

516 10th St, NW, across the street from the theater. Same hours as Ford's Theatre.

The simple three-story brick row house where Lincoln died on April 15, 1865 was built in 1850 by tailor William Petersen. You can visit its three first-floor rooms, which are decorated with Victorian period-furnishings.

Walking with Lincoln

The Ford's Theatre new walking tour series helps history buffs take a step—actually 1.4 miles worth of steps—back in time. The History of Foot series is a 90-minute "walking monologue" where tour leaders trace the story of an individual connected to Abraham Lincoln while stopping at sites significant to the narrative along the way. *Tickets are $12 and can be purchased by calling 202-638-2367 or 800-899-2367.*

HISTORIC SITES

Champion For Civil Rights

Born into slavery in Maryland about 1818, **Frederick Douglass** was the son of a black mother and an unidentified white father. In 1838 Douglass escaped, fled north, and settled in Massachusetts with his wife Anna Murray. In 1841 he became involved with the Massachusetts Anti-Slavery Society and became a respected abolitionist. Soon after the publication of his first book, *Narrative of the Life of Frederick Douglass, An American Slave* (1845), Douglass left for Europe. After the Civil War, Douglass moved to Washington. During his years in Anacostia, Douglass received several presidential appointments to serve in district government. In 1895, after attending a women's rights meeting, Douglass died suddenly of a heart attack at his home.

Frederick Douglass National Historic Site★

1411 W St. SE. 202-426-5961. www.nps.gov/frdo. Open mid-Apr–mid-Oct daily 9am–5pm. Rest of the year daily 9am–4pm. Closed Jan 1, Thanksgiving Day, Dec 25. You can only enter the house on a ranger-led tour. Check the website for times and to make a reservation. (Some same-day tickets available on site.) $2.

Known as Cedar Hill, this white Victorian house was the last residence of black statesman, orator and abolitionist Frederick Douglass. The estate, which tops a shady knoll overlooking the Anacostia River, was originally built as a speculative property in the late 1850s by developer John Van Hook.

When Douglass purchased the nine-acre estate from Van Hook, the house had never been lived in. Douglass expanded the property to 15 acres and added seven rooms to the rear of the house. In 1962 the house was donated to the National Park Service, who restored the estate and opened it to the public as a historic site. Cedar Hill is decorated with Victo-

Frederick Douglass (c. 1879)

National Archives 200(s)FL-22

rian furnishings and memorabilia, most of which belonged to the Douglass family.

The ground floor consists of a formal parlor and a family parlor, a dining room, kitchen, Douglass' study and a pantry and washroom. The five bedrooms on the second floor include those of Douglass and his two successive wives. Behind the house, a small reconstructed stone building served as a second study, which Douglass called "the Growlery."

MUST SEE

Tudor Place★

1644 31st St. NW, two blocks east of Wisconsin Ave. between Q & R Sts. 202-965-0400. www.tudor place.org. Visit by guided tour only, Tue–Sat 10am, 11am, noon, 1pm, 2pm and 3pm; Sun noon–3pm hourly. Closed major holidays. $8.

Here you'll meet the Peter family —six generations of them—who lived in this Georgetown mansion for nearly 180 years. Tudor Place was completed in 1816 as the home of Thomas Peter and his wife, Martha Custis Peter, the granddaughter of Martha Washington.

In 1805, with the $8,000 inheritance Martha Peter received from her step-grandfather, George Washington, the couple purchased an eight-acre city block in Georgetown Heights with sweeping views of the growing capital city and the Potomac River. Dr. William Thornton, a family friend and the first architect of the Capitol, was commissioned to design a stately home that would reflect the Peters' social status. The house, with its distinctive domed portico, took 11 years to build.

At her death in 1854, Martha Peter left the estate to the youngest of the three Peter daughters, Britannia Wellington Peter Kennon, who had been widowed after only a year of marriage. During the Civil War years, Britannia, a staunch Southern sympathizer (and relative of Robert E. Lee), allowed Union officers to use Tudor Place as a boardinghouse, stipulating only that "affairs of war not be discussed" in her presence.

The estate remained in the family until 1983, when it passed to the Tudor Place Foundation. Tudor Place opened to the public in 1988. Today the mansion displays some of the 8,000 household objects that the family owned over the years.

Collections – Highlights include George Washington's Revolutionary War camp stool and Martha Washington's Chippendale tea table from Mount Vernon, as well as a fine collection of 19C European and American silver.

Garden – The 5½ acres of grounds surrounding the house remain just as different generations of the

©Tudor Place Historic House and Garden

South façade, Tudor Place

HISTORIC SITES

Peter family planted them. Here you'll discover a boxwood ellipse, a geometric "knot" of flowers, and the China rose, "Old Blush," that Martha Peter herself planted along the south side of the house.

6th & I Historic Synagogue

600 I Street, NW. 202-408-3100. www.sixthandi.org. Mon–Thu 9am–5pm and Fri 9am–4pm. Tours given the first Sun of the month from 12pm–3pm. (Reservations needed only for groups of 10 or more.) Private tours can be arranged by calling the synagogue. Building closed to the public on most holidays, Sat, and when private events and services are being held.

The 6th and I Historic Synagogue, one of the city's first synagogues, was a liquor license away from becoming a nightclub when three prominent Jewish businessmen swooped in and saved the 1908 landmark at the eleventh hour. Designed by architect Louis Levi, the light gray brick building served as the home to Adas Israel Congregation until 1951, at which time it was sold to the Turner Memorial AME Church when the synagogue relocated to Cleveland Park. In 2002 the director of the Jewish Historical Society of Greater Washington heard the church was selling the building to a nightclub proprietor so it too could relocate its flock.

After a series of hurried phone calls the team of three local businessmen-turned-philanthropists (including Abe Pollin, owner of the Washington Wizards basketball team and the nearby Verizon Center) made a counter offer and purchased the building for $5 million. Following a careful year-long $2 million restoration that relied heavily on photos taken at the synagogue during a 1940s wedding, Sixth & I opened its doors on April 22, 2004.

Today the historic building serves as both a functioning, non-denominational, free community synagogue, welcoming Jewish and non-Jews alike, and a community center that hosts lectures,

6th & I Historic Synagogue

Sixth & I Historic Synagogue

The Octagon★

The building is currently undergoing extensive restoration and is closed to the public. Check the website for updates. 1799 New York Ave., NW. 202-638-3105. www.archfoundation.org. Open year-round Tue–Sun 10am–4pm. Closed Mon, Jan 1, Thanksgiving Day, Dec 25. $5.

What kind of house can you build on a triangular lot? If you're Dr. William Thornton, the first architect of the US Capitol, you build a six-sided one, with three stories. Now owned by the American Architectural Foundation, The Octagon, constructed 1799–1801, ranks as the oldest museum in the US dedicated to architecture and design, and one of America's best examples of Federal-period architecture.

rock concerts, and book talks. The synagogue still has its distinctive, red-tiled roof and the original Corinthian capitals, which stand on columns on either side of the building's entrances. The bimah—the platform from which the Torah is read—had been reconfigured during the building's half-century as a church and was also recreated from old photographs.

All the Torah scrolls currently housed in the Holy Ark and read during services at 6th & I, survived the Holocaust.

The Mary McLeod Bethune Council House

1318 Vermont Avenue NW. 202 673-2402. www.nps.gov/mamc. Mon–Sat from 9am–5pm. Last tour starts at 4pm. Closed Thanksgiving, Christmas, and New Year's Day.

The daughter of former slaves, Mary McLeod Bethune (1875–1955) was a civil rights leader, who worked tirelessly to educate black Americans. In 1904 she founded a school, which is today the Bethune-Cookman University in Daytona. She went on to become a women's rights activist and an advisor to Franklin Roosevelt.

Some of her greatest accomplishments were achieved while living in this townhouse, her last home in Washington, DC. The house also served as the first headquarters of the National Council of Negro Women (NCNW) and now holds the National Archives for Black Women's History. These archives are only available to researchers who book a time slot in advance. (See the website for details.)

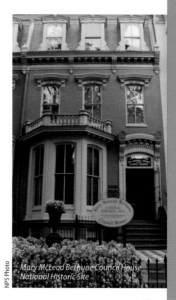

NPS Photo

Mary McLead Bethune Council House National Historic Site

NEIGHBORHOODS

Neighborhoods give a city its character, and DC is no exception. From tony Georgetown to collegiate Foggy Bottom, and from the revitalized Penn Quarter to multi-ethnic Adams Morgan, Washington's neighborhoods all have a unique identity. Here are a few of our favorites.

Georgetown★★

Bounded on the south by the Potomac and on the east by Rock Creek. www.georgetowndc.com.

When Washingtonians think of Georgetown, they usually think shopping during the day and nightlife once the sun goes down. DC's toniest neighborhood contains more than its share of bars and clubs, wonderful restaurants and upscale shopping galore, not

to mention a wealth of historic sights, museums and lovely Federal architecture lining quiet residential streets.

Georgetown began in the early 1700s as the site of a tobacco plantation. Positioned at the head of the Potomac River, the town thrived as a port and as the eastern terminus of the Chesapeake & Ohio Canal (see sidebar, opposite) into the late 18C. It was also during that time (1789) that the first

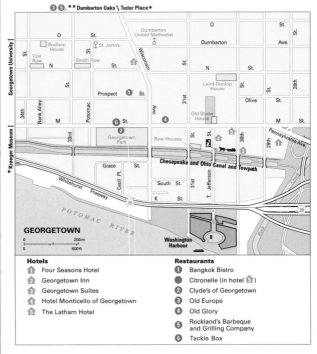

GEORGETOWN

0   200m
0   600ft

Hotels		Restaurants	
Four Seasons Hotel		❶ Bangkok Bistro	
Georgetown Inn		● Citronelle (in hotel 🏨)	
Georgetown Suites		❷ Clyde's of Georgetown	
Hotel Monticello of Georgetown		❸ Old Europe	
The Latham Hotel		❹ Old Glory	
		❺ Rockland's Barbeque and Grilling Company	
		❻ Tackle Box	

MUST SEE

Chesapeake & Ohio Canal National Historical Park

Georgetown visitor center is located at 1057 Thomas Jefferson St. NW, off M St. between 30th & 31st Sts. 202-653-5190. www.nps.gov/choh. Park open daily year-round dawn–dusk.

Part of George Washington's dream to make the Potomac River navigable to western trade, the C&O Canal was intended to span from DC to the Ohio River. Although construction began in 1828, it would be more than 20 years before the "Great Canal Project" would be even partially realized. The project was plagued by constant problems and in 1850 the C&O Canal Company finally gave up. In 1971 President Richard Nixon created the Cheasapeake & Ohio National Historical Park. Today it is the country's only remaining towpath canal.

Catholic institution of higher learning in the country, Georgetown College—now **Georgetown University**—was founded at the western edge of town. Unfortunately for the neighborhood, the efficiency of train travel gradually brought an end to barge transport. At the same time, the advent of steam navigation, which required deeper ports than the town could provide, curtailed Georgetown's shipping business. In 1871 the ailing town was consolidated with the District of Columbia. In the middle part of the last century Georgetown underwent gentrification.

Today Georgetown's residential streets, with their carefully restored Federal-style and mid-19C houses, ooze refinement. You never know who you might see here; many of the city's politicos and foreign dignitaries call this neighborhood home.

What's What In Georgetown

Heart of Georgetown – It all happens along Wisconsin Avenue and M Street, which are lined with myriad restaurants, bars and trendy boutiques. The 14-screen AMC Loews Georgetown on a

©Lillis Photography/iStockphoto.com

Townhouses in Georgetown

Noshing On Connecticut Avenue

A longtime favorite of hungry literature lovers, **Kramerbooks & Afterwords Café** *(1517 Connecticut Ave. NW; 202-387-3825; www.kramers.com)* caters to Washington workaholics with hours from 7am to late-night daily (they're open all night Fri & Sat). Kramerbooks features a full-service bar and live entertainment along with its extensive menu of lunch and dinner fare. **Marvelous Market** *(1511 Connecticut Ave. NW; 202-332-3690; www.marvelous market.com)* is a great place to put together your own carryout meal of homemade soup, pâtés, cheeses, and the market's own superb handmade artisanal breads.

nearby stretch of K Street draws local movie goers from all parts of the city. Along the riverfront, the **Washington Harbour** complex of condos, offices, shops and restaurants incorporates a boardwalk and a terraced fountain court.

Dumbarton Oaks★★ – *1703 32nd St. NW. See Historic Sites.*

Kreeger Museum★ – *2401 Foxhall Rd., NW. See Museums.*

Rock Creek National Park★ – *Nature Center located at 5200 Glover Rd. NW. See Parks and Gardens.*

Tudor Place★ – *1644 31st St. NW. See Historic Sites.*

Dupont Circle★

At the junction of Massachusetts, Connecticut & New Hampshire Aves., and 19th & P Sts. NW.

Favored by business lunchers, chess players and the twenty-something set, this small but vibrant urban park is one of the capital's best people-watching spots. The bustling intersection forms the hub of a chic cosmopolitan neighborhood, which claims many of the city's boutiques and restaurants. Dupont Circle's name honors Civil War hero Rear Admiral Samuel F. du Pont (1803–1865). A bronze statue of du Pont stood in the center of the circle until 1921, when the hero's family

Dupont Circle

Destination DC

moved the memorial to Wilmington, Delaware. Shortly thereafter, the du Ponts replaced the statue with the marble fountain that now graces the circle. It was designed in 1921 by Daniel Chester French. Today the circle itself has become a popular place for locals to grab some fresh air during lunch and for students and visitors to check email (the circle has free Wi-Fi) and read during the day.

The Phillips Collection★★ –
1600 21st St. NW. See Museums.
Society of the Cincinnati/ Anderson House Museum★ –
2118 Massachusetts Ave. NW. 202-785-2040. Open year-round Tue–Sat 1pm–4pm. Closed major holidays. www.societyofthecincinnati.org.
The headquarters of this patriotic society, founded in 1783 by former Revolutionary War officers, displays war artifacts and an array of fine art collected by its previous owners, Larz and Isabel Anderson.

Foggy Bottom★

Between Lafayette Square and Georgetown, south of Dupont Circle.

Now home to George Washington University, the **John F. Kennedy Center for the Performing Arts★★** *(see Performing Arts)* and the infamous Watergate condominium complex, this area

west of the White House was once fog-shrouded bottomland. Breweries, glass plants and the city gas works sprang up here in the early 19C, when the area was home to a mix of Irish, Germans and African Americans. Waterfront warehouses, wharves and rows of narrow brick tenements added to the district's industrial character. In 1912 **George Washington University** moved to the northern end of Foggy Bottom, bringing a collegiate air to the streets southeast of Washington Circle. After World War II, Foggy Bottom developed as an administrative quarter. Among the organizations located here today are the Department of the Interior, the Department of State, and the National Academy of Sciences.

Embassy Row

Massachusetts Ave., between Scott Circle & Observatory Circle. Consulates are open for official business only. For a complete list of embassies in Washington, DC, check online at www.embassy.org.

Embassy Row is the popular name of the two-mile portion of Massachusetts Avenue between Scott Circle and Observatory Circle where you'll find the greatest concentration of DC's many embassies. You'll recognize the

---

Textile Museum★

2320 S St. NW. 202-667-0441. www.textilemuseum.org. Open year-round Mon–Sat 10am–5pm, Sun 1pm–5pm. Closed Dec 24 & 25, & major holidays.

If you're into handmade Oriental rugs, check out the Textile Museum while you're in the Embassy Row neighborhood. Started by George Hewitt Myers in 1925, this small private museum boasts a collection of 17,000 rugs and textiles, dating back to 3,000 BC.

NEIGHBORHOODS

R. Corbel/Michelin

No. 2315 Massachusetts Avenue

chanceries (the embassies proper) and the ambassadors' residences (which may be separate from the chanceries) by the colorful flags or plaques that decorate their facades. The 2mi stretch of Massachusetts Avenue from 22nd Street to Observatory Circle is considered the most distinctive and elegant segment of Embassy Row. It developed with palatial homes in the first decade of the 20th century. After the 1929 stock-market crash, the area's residents were forced to move to more modest quarters and foreign governments began buying up the mansions. The **Islamic Center of Washington DC** *(2551 Massachusetts Ave NW, 202-332-8343, www.theislamiccenter.com)*, a mosque and cultural center, also makes its home on Embassy Row. Prayer services are held daily inside the beautiful white limestone building, which features delicate arches, intricate tile work, and a 162-foot-high minaret.

Penn Quarter

Between 3rd St. on the east and 15th St. on the west, Pennsylvania Ave. on the south and New York and Massachusetts Aves. on the north.

When hip Washingtonians want to see or be seen they head to Penn Quarter—or better yet they make one of its new lofts their return address. A neighborhood that grew up from a forgotten part of town, Penn Quarter began its transformation around 1997 with the opening of the Verizon Center, then called the MCI Center. Funky restaurants, whimsical shops, trendy art galleries, boutique hotels, and luxury apartment buildings (many that have kept elements of the original 19th century architecture) started sprouting up around it. The Pennsylvania Avenue Development Corporation's "Pennsylvania Avenue Plan" to create a mixed-use neighborhood in the East End of downtown helped spark the change. Today Penn Quarter attracts visitors and locals around the clock and is a sought after place to live. The neighborhood touts a long list of highlights including the Interna-

Islamic Center

©Simon Pulsifer/Wikimedia Commons

tional Spy Museum, the National Portrait Gallery, the Shakespeare Theatre Company, the U.S. Navy Memorial, and the National Building Museum. A late-night bowling alley, multiplex and art film movie house are other big draws. On Thursday afternoons from mid-Apr–mid-Dec, the popular FRESHFARM's **Penn Quarter farmers market** *(along 8th St., just south of E St.; 202-362-8889; www. freshfarmmarkets.org)* sells locally grown produce, cheeses, breads, cookies, meat, pastries, soaps, plants and flowers.

Upper Northwest DC (Cleveland Park and Woodley Park)

Woodley Park is bounded on the north by Woodley and Klingle Rds., on the east by the National Zoo and Rock Creek Park, on the south by Calvert St., and on the west by 34th St. Cleveland Park is bounded by Rock Creek Park to the east, Wisconsin and Idaho Avenues to the west, Klingle and Woodley Rds. to the south, and Rodman and Tilden Sts. to the north.

Connecticut Avenue serves as the heart of this part of town. Easy access to the Metro's Red Line makes both the Woodley Park/National Zoo and Cleveland Park neighborhoods popular choices for many who want to live in the city but don't quite want the full urban experience of downtown. The stretch of Connecticut Ave. surrounding the Woodley Park stop is lined with early 20th century rowhouses that now play host to a smorgasbord of international restaurants ranging from Afghani to Thai. Two of the city's largest

hotels, the Marriott Wardman Park and Omni Shoreham, are here. In early spring the large garden in front of the Marriott bursts with color as hundreds upon hundreds of tulips bloom creating magnificent floral eye candy for those who hurry down Connecticut Avenue. Cleveland Park has as its own share of restaurants ranging from small independent take-out spots to fine dining. Apartment buildings, including Joseph Younger's art deco masterpiece the Kennedy-Warren *(3133 Conn. Ave., NW)*, dot the avenue while pretty private homes can be found on the nearby tree-lined side streets. The **National Zoo** sits midway between the Woodley Park and Cleveland Park stops.

Although Woodley Park/National Zoo carries the attraction's name, locals know to get off at Cleveland Park and walk south rather than tackle the steep hill that leads up to the zoo from the Woodley Park station.

Historic Theater

Residents of Cleveland Park take tremendous pride in their local movie theater, the **AMC Loews Uptown 1** *(3426 Conn. Ave NW)*. The city's only remaining movie palace, the art deco Uptown was designed by Baltimore architect John J. Zink and opened for business in 1936. The World Premiere of 2001: A Space Odyssey took place at the Uptown Theater on April 2, 1968. The historic theater's 70-foot-wide screen and balcony with stadium seating still packs in a crowd and the occasional red carpet premiere.

NEIGHBORHOODS

PARKS AND GARDENS

Visiting all those museums, memorials and historic sights can get exhausting. Why not take a break and drink in the flowery sights and recreational activities in DC's most inviting parks and tranquil gardens?

US Botanic Garden★★

On the Mall along 1st St., between Maryland Ave. & C St. 202-225-8333. www.usbg.gov. Conservatory open year-round daily 10am–5pm.

A plant conservatory across from the Capitol? Sure, there's been a botanic garden there since 1850, when the collection of exotic specimens brought from the South Seas by a team of US explorers was housed on the Mall. Begun in 1931, the present conservatory, boasts a state-of-the-art automated environmental-control system. The nation's living-plant museum showcases some 4,000 specimens, including seasonal floral exhibits, towering subtropical plants and flowering orchids. Situated across Independence Avenue, the formal plantings at **Bartholdi Park** provide a colorful setting for the cast-iron **Bartholdi Fountain**, sculpted by Frédéric-Auguste Bartholdi, creator of the Statue of Liberty. The $10 million

National Garden opened to the public in 2006. This project was solely funded by private donations. It includes a three-acre public garden and an environmental learning center.

National Arboretum★

3501 New York Ave. NE. Other entrance at 24th & R Sts. NE. 202-245-2726. www.usna.usda.gov. Grounds open year-round daily 8am–5pm. Closed Dec 25.

If you happen to be visiting DC in late spring, make the National Arboretum a must-see. Here you'll find thousands of **azaleas**, setting the garden's hillsides ablaze with color. One of the country's largest arboretums, this federally owned 446-acre tract is an oasis in the midst of the warehouses of the surrounding area. Established by Congress in 1927, the arboretum did not become a reality until 1947, when the first azaleas were planted. Washingtonians couldn't resist the blooming shrubs and local enthusiasm spurred the gardens to go public in 1954. Today the arboretum's hills and valleys are covered in a variety of blooms.

Garden Delights
National Bonsai and Penjing Museum★ – *Open daily 10am–4pm, closed most major holidays.* The walled Japanese garden complex, behind the modern administration building, includes the Penjing Museum,

US Botanic Garden

Gwen Cannon/Michelin

Touring Tips

The arboretum is designed to be toured by car. Nine miles of paved roads lead past the gardens and plant collections; parking areas are designated along the route. Another option is the 40-minute open-air tram tour, which gives you a history of the gardens as well as a look at the highlights *(mid-Apr–mid-Oct weekends only, 10:30am (if not reserved), 1pm, 2pm, 3pm & 4pm (in peak season only); $4).*

renowned for its outstanding collection of Japanese, Chinese and American bonsai.

Herb Garden – This two-acre garden features a formal 16C English knot garden; a rose garden with more than 80 varieties of antique roses; and 10 specialty gardens, where herbs are grouped according to their historic uses.

National Capitol Columns – Set atop a bluff, these columns originally flanked the east entrance of the Capitol building prior to its expansion in the late 1950s.

Rock Creek National Park★

Nature Center located at 5200 Glover Rd. NW. 202-895-6070. www.nps.gov/rocr. Park open year-round daily dawn–dusk. Nature Center open Wed–Sun 9am–5pm; closed major holidays.

The capital's largest recreational area, Rock Creek Park covers some 2,100 acres astride scenic Rock Creek in Northwest DC. You can easily while away a day here. Start at the **Nature Center**, where you can get maps and information about what's going on in the park. This is also where many of the ranger-led programs start.

A network of paved roads, hiking trails, and bicycle and bridle paths crisscross the vast park.

There are also dozens of picnic areas, tennis courts, and fields. At the outdoor **Carter Barron Amphitheater** *(16th St. & Colorado Ave. NW; 202-426-0486),* you can catch summer concerts and performances.

History In The Park
Old Stone House – *3051 M. St. NW. Open Wed–Sun.* This 1765 stone house in Georgetown exemplifies the life lived by DC's ordinary citizens in colonial days.
Peirce Mill – *Off Tilden St. NW, just west of Beach Dr.* Built in the 1820s, the mill operated on and off until 1993. Currently Peirce Mill is closed until funds can be raised for its repair.
Battleground National Cemetery – *6625 Georgia Ave.* This Civil War burial ground was established in July 1864, following the Battle of Fort Stevens.

Horsing Around

With its 13mi of bridle paths, the park makes a great place to ride. Located next to the Nature Center, the Rock Creek Park Horse Center offers riding lessons, guided trail rides, and pony rides for the wee ones. There's even an equitation field in the park. For information, call the Horse Center *(202-362-0117; www.rock creekhorsecenter.com).*

PARKS AND GARDENS

81

FOR FUN

In a city that boasts the country's largest concentration of PhDs, you have to wonder what they do for fun here. Never fear, DC has more than its share of outdoor activities and quirky tours to amuse you once you get bored with all the serious stuff.

Bike the Sites

Main location is on 12th St., NW, between Pennsylvania and Constitution Aves. (202) 842-2453. www.bikethesites.com. $32–$45.

See the sites and get in your cardio at the same time. Bike the Sites offers several different bicycle tours including "Blossoms by Bike" in the spring and a "Ghost Bike Tour" in October. Bicycles, helmets, water and a snack are included in the cost of the guided tour. The company also rents bikes if you want to go out and explore the city on your own.

C&O Canal Barge Ride

Rides ($5) depart May–mid-Nov Wed–Sun from the C&O Canal National Historical Park visitor center in Georgetown. 1057 Thomas Jefferson St. NW. For schedules, call 202-653-5190. www.nps.gov/choh.

Travel back in time on a mule-drawn canal boat (The Chesapeake and Ohio Canal maintains a stable of six to eight mules for its canal boat operations). Guides in mid-19C period costume will tell you the story of the canal and what life was like in Georgetown's early days.

During the hour-long trip down the Georgetown section of the C&O, you'll get to go through one of the canal's original lock lifts.

Golf

DC claims several public golf courses including the **East Potomac Park Golf Course** *(972 Ohio Dr, SW, 202-554-7660)*, the **Langston Golf Course & Driving Range** *(2600 Benning Rd, NE, 202-397-8638)* and **Rock Creek Golf Course** *(16th & Rittenhouse, NW, 202 882-7332)*. Public facilities at East Potomac Park include 3 public golf courses, a mini-golf course,

Bike tours

Destination DC

Barge ride on the C & O Canal

©William Perry/Bigstockphoto.com

a driving range, a playground, tennis courts, picnic facilities, and a recreation center. The southern end of the park is known as Hains Point. All of the facilities rent clubs and other equipment.

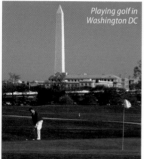

Playing golf in Washington DC

Destination DC

Gravelly Point

North of the runway at Ronald Reagan Washington National Airport in Arlington, VA. Use the northbound lanes on the GW Parkway toward the airport— there is no southbound access.

Can't help but look up when you hear the roar of jet? Does your heart skip a beat when you hear the numbers 777? Do you secretly think of airports as more of a destination than part of the journey? If you answered yes to any of these questions—or if you just get a kick out of airplanes—then you'll feel right at home at Gravelly Point. The park, on the shore of the Potomac River right next to Reagan National Airport, is considered by many aviation enthusiasts to be one of the best places in the country for plane spotting. Standing at the park it sounds and feels like you can touch the low-flying aircraft coming in for a landing. (Make sure you snap the requisite photo of you reaching up to touch the jets.) During busy times planes zoom above every few minutes. Visitors can also enjoy Gravelly Point's big lawn near the water and great view of the city.

Hike or Bike the C&O Canal Towpath to Old Angler's Inn

Pick up the towpath in George-town, ½ block south of M St. between 29th & 35th Sts. NW. For information, stop at the **C&O Canal National Historical Park** visitor center (*1057 Thomas*

83

Jefferson St. NW; off M St. between 30th & 31st Sts; 202-653-5190; www.nps.gov/choh).

A quiet walk or bike ride along the old **C&O Canal towpath** will give you exercise with a view of both lovely scenery and the area's historic past (see Neighborhoods/ Georgetown). From Georgetown, follow the towpath about 12mi north. Between mile marker 12 and 13, you'll find the **Old Angler's Inn**, a wonderful place to rest and have lunch or a drink on the outdoor terrace. The rustic inn, which has been serving travelers along the canal route since 1860, now features excellent New American cuisine (10801 MacArthur Blvd., Potomac, MD; 301-299-9097; www.oldanglersinn.com; open for lunch & dinner Tue–Sun).

National Sculpture Garden—Fun For All Seasons

On the Mall at 7th St. & Constitution Ave. NW. 202-737-4215. www.nga.gov.

In summer and winter, you'll find fun afoot at the National Gallery of Art's Sculpture Garden. Every Friday night (5pm–8:30pm, rain or shine) in summer, there are free **jazz concerts** in front of the Pavilion Café, which stays open during performances.

A favorite with Washingtonians, **ice-skating** on the Sculpture Garden's rink is a great way to spend a chilly winter afternoon or evening (on the Mall at Madison Dr. & 9th St. NW; open mid-Nov–mid-Mar, weather permitting; Mon–Thu 10am–11pm, Fri & Sat 10am–midnight, Sun 11am–9pm; $6/2hr session; skate rental $2.50, photo

ID required). Two blocks from the White House, Pershing Park Ice Rink (14th & Pennsylvania Avenues, NW) also lets you skate with a view ($6.50 for Adults, $5.50 for Children 12 and under, and $2.50 for skate rental). If you're in the city at Christmastime, be sure to walk over to the Ellipse (Constitution Ave. between 15th & 17th Sts. NW) after your skating session to see the National Christmas tree.

On Location Tours

Saturdays at 10am. www.screen tours.com. Meets near Union Station—exact location provided once tickets are purchased tickets. $32.

Want to sip a drink at the St. Elmo's Fire bar? Climb the steps of The Exorcist house? See the real life props used by your favorite West Wing characters? If so, then On Location DC has got your name on it. The 3-hour local-actor-led bus tour takes visitors on a fun romp through the real-life sites captured on film in dozens of famous movies and television shows.

Outdoor Movies

Screen on the Green: The screen is located off of Constitution Ave, between 4th & 7th Streets, NW. 877-262-5866. www.nps.gov/ nama. NoMA Summer Film Festival: at the intersection of New York Avenue and Florida Avenues, NE, 202-289 -0111. www.georgetown filmfest.com.

The National Mall serves as the backdrop to many a protest and festivals and, during the summer months, to classic films. Every Monday night during the long days of summer, **Screen on the Green** shows free flicks on an enormous movie screen placed among the monuments. Showings begin at sunset (around 8pm) but people arrive earlier to secure a good spot. Bring a blanket, a picnic basket (minus any alcohol which is prohibited) and enjoy movies like Dr. No, The Apartment and Superman. Movies play except in extreme weather. NoMA Summer Film Festival

During the summer The NoMa (North of Massachusetts Avenue) Business Improvement District also hosts a free summer-long outdoor film festival in Northeast DC. A campy vibe sets the tone for the festival. Bond, James Bond, was the star of all 16 films in 2008. The audience got in the mood for all things 007 by cheering on contestants in the Oddjob look-alike contest as they attempted to toss their bowler hats onto statues. Clint Eastwood took top billing in 2007. Movies begin at dusk.

Paddle or cruise the Potomac River

Rentals available at Thompson Boat Center, 2900 Virginia Ave., at the corner of Rock Creek Pkwy. in Georgetown. 202-333-9543. www.thompsonboatcenter.com. Rentals available mid-Mar–Oct (water has to be above 55 degrees) daily 8am–6pm. Rentals start at $8hr.

If you're hankering to get out on the water, you can rent canoes and kayaks by the hour or by the day at **Thompson Boat Center**. From Thompson's it's an easy paddle to Roosevelt Island *(below)* or the Georgetown waterfront. Landlubbers can rent bikes here, too

Kayaking on the Potomac River

(mid-Mar–Sept) for a ride along the C&O Canal towpath or the Rock Creek Park bike path *(see Parks and Gardens)*. If you're not quite feeling energetic enough, take a sightseeing cruise on the river. Check out the special cruises from **Potomac Riverboat company** *(www.potomacriverboatco.com)* who organise canine cruises for your four legged friends or pirate cruises for the kids.

Rock Creek Park Horse Center

Just off Military Road, on Glover Road, NW, (next door to The Nature Center in Rock Creek Park). 202-362-0117. www.rockcreek horsecenter.com. Tue–Fri noon–6pm and 9am–5pm on weekends. Closed Mondays, Thanksgiving Day, Christmas Day and New Year's Day.

If you need a break from all the marble statues and painted masterpieces head over to Rock Creek Park's equestrian center and

FOR FUN

visit with the horses or maybe even take a ride. Guided trail rides ($35 for one hour) and pony rides for children ($20 for 15 minutes) are given in spring, summer and early fall. Reservations are a must as there are a limited number of ride slots each week and they tend to fill up quickly. You don't have to have any riding experience to participate but you do have to wear the helmet the center provides and compliment your horse as you trot through the park.

Scandal Tour

Departs from the Old Post Office Pavilion at 1100 Pennsylvania Ave, NW Jul–Labor Day, Sat 1pm. Reservations required. 202-783-7212. www.gnpcomedy.com. $30.

What skeletons lurk in the White House closets? What Congressman took a moonlight skinny-dip in the Tidal Basin with stripper Fannie Fox? You'll find out the answers to these probing questions and more on the hilarious two-hour Scandal Tour, led by members of DC's Gross National Product comedy troupe. And you can count on there always being something new to see, because in this town, there's always a scandal brewing. (Tip: Leave the kids at home for this one.)

Spydrive

For groups only. Your ticket will instruct you where to meet your tour leader. Reservations required. 800-779-4007 or 703-642-7450. www.spytrek.com. Price depends on how many people in your group.

You'll never look at Washington, DC the same way again after you take this 2½-hour undercover tour. Led by former intelligence officers from the FBI, CIA and Russia's KGB, Spydrive takes you on a bus past sites where real spies lived, worked and operated. You'll see dead drops, signal sites and meeting places—and you thought the capital's monuments were just historic sites! A full day course for DC was just added. We'd tell you the details but then we'd have to kill you...

Swimming

The DC Department of Recreation operates several indoor and outdoor pools throughout the city. Most are open to non-residents for a minimal fee. Log on to http://dpr.dc.gov for a full list and operating hours. Most hotel pools are for guests only but a few sell summer memberships.

If you're traveling with kids and DC's humidity is wilting you, head over the border to the **Water Mine Family Swimmin' Hole** *(1400 Lake Fairfax in Reston, VA 20190; 703-471-5415)*. Operated by the Fairfax County Park Authority, this splash park offers slides, flumes, sprays, and showers as far as the eye can see.

MUST DO

City Segway Tours

City Segway Tours

624 9th Street, NW (between F and G Sts across from the National Portrait Gallery). 202-626-0017 or 877-734-8687. www.citysegway tours.com. Daytime tours at 10am and 2pm everyday. Evening tours everyday at 6pm. $70.

You can literally roll through the town on a guided City Segway tour. These self-balancing, personal transportation devices are a fun way to cover a lot of ground without hoping on and off a tour bus. They're also guaranteed to get you a few double takes from the unsuspecting pedestrians sharing the sidewalk. Tours run 3 hours and cruise by all the downtown highlights including the Supreme Court, the White House and the Washington Monument. You must be at least 16 years old to ride.

Theodore Roosevelt Island

Access only from the northbound lanes of George Washington Memorial Pkwy. From DC, take George Washington Pkwy. north past the exit for Key Bridge; the island will be on your right. Park and walk across the footbridge. No bicycles permitted. Park is open from dawn until dusk. 703-289-2500. www.nps.gov/this.

A striking statue of President Theodore Roosevelt greets you as you enter this 91-acre woodland preserve, which makes a fitting memorial to the conservationist for whom it's named. Located near Arlington, Virginia, the forested island on the Potomac River is threaded by 2½mi of nature trails. Take a peaceful walk through the woodlands and marshes, where you'll see a variety of wildlife, especially birds. You can fish here, too, but permits are required for anyone over 16.

FOR KIDS

Despite the policy-making and other serious doings that go on in this city, DC likes to kid around. In fact, many of its Very Important People are still young at heart. These picks are guaranteed to please "kids" of all ages. And best of all, many of them are free!

National Air and Space Museum★★★

On the Mall at Independence Ave. & 6th St. SW. 202-633-1000. www.nasm.si.edu. For hours, see Museums.

The world's most-visited museum is a sure-fire hit with kids. From IMAX movies to lunar modules, it's all about flying. See the Wright Brothers 1903 Flyer and Lindbergh's Spirit of St. Louis. Touch a moon rock. Imagine what it would be like to hurtle through earth's atmosphere in a cramped space capsule. Big kids will want to take a turn at the Flight Simulator Zone. In this simulator 12 feet above the ground, you control the gut-wrenching barrel rolls, upside-down loops, and other aerobatic feats, enhanced by a 58-inch virtual-reality screen and high-tech sound effects.

National Zoological Park★★

3001 Connecticut Ave. NW. Other entrance on Beach Dr. 202-633-4800. www.natzoo.si.edu. Grounds open Apr–Oct daily 6am–8pm; buildings open 10am–6pm. Rest of the year grounds close at 6pm; buildings close at 4:30pm. Closed Dec 25.

Plan at least a half-day to see this 163-acre urban zoo, set in the northern section of Rock Creek Park. Housing some 28,000 animals representing 435 different species, the zoo was created in 1887 as the Department of Living Animals, and was originally located on the Mall. In 1889 Congress appropriated funds for the creation of a true zoological park, to be administered by the Smithsonian Institution. A 163-acre tract above Rock Creek Park was purchased,

Charles Lindbergh's Spirit of St. Louis, SpaceShipOne and Chuck Yeager's Bell X-1 in Milestones Gallery

Photo by Eric Long, National Air and Space Museum, Smithsonian Institution

MUST DO

Giant pandas, Tian Tian and Mei Xiang in Panda House

Jessie Cohen, Smithsonian's National Zoo

and renowned landscape architect Frederick Law Olmsted laid out plans for the new zoo. Now revamped and modernized, the zoo continues its mission to "study, celebrate and protect animals and their habitats."

What's Hot At The Zoo?

Panda House★★ – This is the home of the zoo's most popular inhabitants, Giant Pandas Tian Tian and Mei Xiang.

African Savanna★ – The savanna re-creates the dry tropical East African grassland, where lions and cheetahs coexist with hippos, zebras and gazelles.

Kids' Farm★★ – Young children love the barn and farm animals that make their home in the Kid's Farm. At the Caring Corral, children have a chance to help groom goats and donkeys with the help of the zoo staff.

Think Tank★ – The zoo's oldest building (1906) now contains exhibits that detail animal thought processes and communication skills. Watch keepers teach symbolic language to resident orangutans, who commute between the Think Tank and the Great Ape House via vine-like cables suspended 20 feet over the zoo's pathways.

Reptile Discovery Center – The 1929 Byzantine-style center houses the world's largest lizard, the Komodo dragon, along with other lizards and a host of snakes.

DC's Darlings

In 1972, the zoo's first breeding pair of Giant Pandas, Hsing Hsing and Ling Ling, captured the hearts of Washingtonians, who came to see them by the thousands. No less popular are the newest pair, Tian Tian (b. 1997) and Mei Xiang (b. 1998), who arrived in the US from China in December 2000. The pandas quickly made themselves at home in their new habitat and on July 9, 2005, Mei Xiang gave birth to Tai Shan. People waited in line for hours to see the cub. The People's Republic of China receives $1 million per year for the loan of the pandas; these funds will assist efforts to preserve the wild panda population.

FOR KIDS

ImaginAsia at the Sackler Gallery★★

On the Mall at 1050 Independence Ave. SW. Programs are held in the classroom on the 2nd floor of the gallery. 202-357-2700. www.asia. si.edu. For hours, see Museums.

Art doesn't have to be boring. At the Sackler and at its sister museum, the Freer Gallery★★ *(Jefferson Dr. at 12th St. SW; 202-357-4880)*, families can tour the exhibits with the help of a self-guided tour booklet, courtesy of the museum's ImaginAsia program. After you've toured the exhibit, the kids (ages 8–14) can make their own art project based on what they saw. Children must be accompanied by an adult.

National Museum of Natural History★★

On the Mall at 10th St & Constitution Ave. NW. 202-357-2700. www.nmnh.si.edu. For hours, see Museums.

Goldilocks may have thought the wolf's teeth were big, but they were nothing compared to the choppers on the museum's Tyrannosaurus rex. T-rex is joined by buddies "Hatcher" the triceratops and an 90-foot-long Diplodocus in the first-floor Dinosaurs exhibit. Scared of big things? The Insect Zoo (2nd floor) has lots of little things—it's just that some of them are pretty creepy. See an ant colony, touch a tarantula (if you dare!) and find out why your home and yard are favorite hangouts for insect critters.

Check out the tarantula feedings *(Tue–Fri 10:30am, 11:30am & 1:30pm; weekends 11:30am, 12:30pm & 1:30pm).*

For a less creepy crawly experience, get tickets for **The Butterfly Pavilion** and take a stroll among hundreds of live butterflies and exotic plants. Tickets cost $6 for adults and $5 for kids. Tuesdays are free but tickets are still required. *Daily 10:15am–5pm. Check website or call 202-633-4629.*

Spark!Lab at National Museum of American History★★

Constitution Ave., between 12th & 14th Sts. NW. 202-633-1000. www.americanhistory.si.edu. Open Tue–Fri 12:30pm–5pm, weekends 10am–5pm (hours are subject to change; call to check before you visit).

Young visitors can charge their imagination at the Spark!Lab, a hands-on-science and invention center for all ages; see the enchanting Dolls' House with its 23 rooms; view Kermit the Frog

Kermit the Frog, National Museum of American History

National Museum of American History

Carousel on the Mall

and Dumbo, the Flying Elephant, from Disneyland; as well as "ride" a Chicago Transit Authority car in America on the Move. Touch stations located in exhibitions and along the new artifact wall displays will engage children in hands-on activities—such as cranking up a cotton gin.

Carousel on the Mall

On the Mall, in front of the Arts & Industries Building (between the Smithsonian Castle and the Hirshhorn Gallery). Phone 202-633-1000 or 202-633-5285 . www.si.edu. Open Mar–early Sept daily 10am–5:30pm. Rest of the year daily 11am–5pm. Closed Dec 25. $2.

Who can resist a carousel? A ride on a beautiful 1947 carousel, which still goes 'round and 'round on the Mall, is a great way to give the kids—and maybe you, too—a break from museum-going.

Discovery Theater at the Smithsonian

In the Arts & Industries Building, 900 Jefferson Dr. SW. 202-633-8700. www.discoverytheater.org. Open Sept–Jul Mon–Fri 10am & 11:30am. No shows in Aug. $5 adults, $4 children.

From African rhythms to magic shows, Discovery Theater entertains the younger set with puppets, storytellers, actors, dancers, musicians, and mimes. This ongoing series of live performances especially for kids features a dozen performances each season. With themes including international folk tales and American history, your child just may learn something, too despite all the fun.

Imagination Stage

4908 Auburn Avenue Bethesda, Maryland. 301.280.1660. Box office: 301-280-1660.

Dazzle your young thespian with a performance at Bethesda's much-loved Imagination Stage where the shows and production

©Kathleen R. Grilley/Bigstockphoto.com

FOR KIDS

91

value rival anything you would see downtown. The Bethesda arts center and theater is devoted to children. In the Lerner Family Theatre professional productions wow the juice box set and the center's second stage, the Christopher and Dana Reeve Studio Theatre, is where student productions take place. The café serves up lunch and cookies that tie in with the theme of the current show; the gift shop and its dress up collection can be hard to pass by. Each September Imagination Stage holds a free activity-filled open house.

National Aquarium

14th St. & Constitution Ave. NW. 202-482-2825. www.national aquarium.com. Open year-round daily 9am–5pm. Closed Dec 25 and Thanksgiving. $7 adults, $3 children.

This small aquarium, established in 1873, ranks as the nation's oldest. Tanks here swim with some 1,500 specimens of marine life. Look for sharks, piranhas, sea turtles, moray eels, sea horses and toadfish, among a host of other denizens of the deep. Don't miss the daily talks and feedings (2pm) by animal keepers at the aquarium.

National Geographic Society Explorer's Hall

17th & M Sts. NW. 202-857-7588. www.nationalgeographic.com/explorer. Open year-round Mon–Sat 9am–5pm, Sun 10am–5pm. Closed Dec 25.

Kids love these interactive exhibits, done as only the Geographic can do them. In the recent past, visitors

to Explorer's Hall have been able to meet Dinosaurs of the Sahara; explore the ends of the earth with Sir Edmund Hillary, Everest and Beyond; and visit a Robot Zoo. New experiences are waiting for you!

Paddleboats on the Tidal Basin

At the west end of the Mall, just south of the Washington Monument.

No visit to DC is complete without a turn around the Tidal Basin in a paddleboat on a sunny day. You can rent boats by the hour from the **Tidal Basin Boat House** *(15th St. & Maine Ave. SW; open Mar–Sept daily 10am–6pm; $8/hr for 2-passenger boat, $16/hr for 4-passenger boat; 202-484-0206; photo ID required).* This is great fun for the whole family.

Puppet Co. Playhouse

At Glen Echo Park, off MacArthur Blvd. in Glen Echo, MD. 301-320-6668. www.thepuppetco.org. Performances year-round Wed, Thu & Fri 10am & 11:30am, weekends 11:30am & 1pm. $8 (free for children under 2).

What kid doesn't like puppet shows? Since 1989 the 200-seat playhouse in Glen Echo Park has been staging puppet productions for children. The 20-show repertory includes such classics as The Velveteen Rabbit, Jungle Book and The Nutcracker. A combination of hand puppets, body puppets, shadow puppets, rod puppets and marionettes is used in the productions, which change about every six weeks.

PERFORMING ARTS

While Washington, DC conjures up images of political debates and daily crises on the House floor, government officials aren't the only ones making scenes around the nation's capital. Don't let the city's straight-laced atmosphere fool you—from symphonies to pop stars, DC knows how to put on a show. Round up your chorus line and head out to these top performance spots.

Grand Foyer, John F. Kennedy Center for the Performing Arts

John F. Kennedy Center

John F. Kennedy Center★★

New Hampshire Ave. at Rock Creek Pkwy. NW. Guided tours available. Tickets and information: 202-467-4600 or 800-444-1324. www.kennedy-center.org.

A gleaming horizontal mass, ranking as one of the country's leading cultural institutions, this "living memorial" to the 35th US president is home to the National Symphony Orchestra. A wide spectrum of world-class entertainment—from tenor Placido Domingo to comedian Bill Cosby to Broadway's The Lion King—is offered in its six theaters. When you enter the 630-foot-long Grand Foyer, with its prominent bronze bust of President Kennedy, you'll be awed by the 60-foot-high mirrors from Belgium and the eighteen crystal chandeliers from Sweden. Free public performances take place every day of the year at 6pm on Millennium Stage in the Grand Foyer. Gaze skyward at the collection of flags in the **Hall of States** and the **Hall of Nations** and treat yourself to some extra Milk Duds at the concession stand if you can correctly identify them all.

Ford's Theatre★

10th St., between E & F Sts. NW. www.fordstheatre.org. Guided tours available: 202-426-6924. Tickets: 202-347-4833. For description, see Historic Sites.

John Wilkes Booth's assassination of President Abraham Lincoln in 1865 quickly put Ford's Theatre on the map. Afterwards, as national chaos ensued, a curtain fell on theatrical productions for nearly a hundred years, until a restoration effort began in the 1960s. Today, Ford's Theatre thrives again as a living tribute to Lincoln's passion for the performing arts. American life takes center stage in productions ranging from musicals to star-studded TV specials to classic dramas. The historic theater is undergoing a full-scale renovation and will reopen in 2009.

PERFORMING ARTS

Low On Cash?

Get discounted day-of-show tickets at **TICKETplace** *(407 7th St. NW; open Tue–Fri 11am–6pm, Sat 11am–5pm; 202-842-5387; www.ticketplace.org.)*
They offer half-price ticket sales for most performances in Washington, DC when available. Check the website for a listing of current and some advance sales.

Arena Stage

Temporary theater location:1800 S. Bell Street, Arlington, VA 22202. Arena is also using Lincoln Theatre, located at 1215 U Street, NW, during construction. All tickets: 202 -488-3300. www.arena-stage.org.

As the first nonprofit theater in the US (c. 1950), Arena Stage has been synonymous with artistic expression and diversity. Arena presents both classic and contemporary theatrical pieces; recent offerings have included Molière's Misanthrope and Mrs. Bob Cratchit's Wild Christmas Binge. The theater is currently in the middle of construction and fundraising for a new three-stage facility. The new Arena Stage will be part of the Mead Center for American Theater. It is scheduled to be completed for the 2010/2011 season.

National Theatre

1321 Pennsylvania Ave. NW. 202-628-6161. Tickets: 800-447-7400. www.nationaltheatre.org.

What do Warren Beatty and Shirley MacLaine have in common? Besides being brother and sister, they both worked at the National (Warren as a doorman, Shirley as an usher) before becoming stars in their own right. Just three blocks from the White House, the "Theatre of Presidents" stages blockbuster traveling Broadway shows like Cats! and The Wizard of Oz.

Shakespeare Theatre

450 7th St. NW. 202-547-1122 or 877.487.8849. www.shakespeare dc.org. Season runs Sept–Jun.

One of the nation's most acclaimed theatrical companies presents works by Shakespeare and other classical playwrights in this readaptation of the old Landsburgh department store. Formerly located at the Folger Library, the theatre moved to this revitalized area in 1992 and continues building its excellent reputation in both the Lansburgh Theatre and the new Sidney Harman Hall.

Warner Theatre

13th & E Sts. NW. 202-783-4000. Tickets: 800-551-7328. www.warnertheatre.com.

The Warner began in the vaudeville days of the Roaring Twenties. By 1945, the theatre had adopted a movies-only policy, and offered everything from classics like Ben Hur to pornographic films in the 1970s. After extensive renovations, Warner Theatre reemerged in 1992. It continues to draw top recording artists and a full array of dance and theatrical productions.

🎭 Wolf Trap Farm Park

1645 Trap Rd., off Rte. 7 in Vienna, VA. 703-255-1900. Tickets: 877-965-3872. www.wolf-trap.org.

Grab a picnic dinner and a blanket and settle back under the stars. From Beethoven to the Beach Boys, the Wolf Trap Foundation in nearby northern Virginia presents a kaleidoscope of performances, including dance, theater and its own opera company. The Filene Center outdoor amphitheater seats 7,000, while The Barns accommodate 352 people for more intimate indoor stagings.

Woolly Mammoth

641 D St NW. 202-289-2443. Tickets: 202-393-3939. www.woollymammoth.net.

American values may be upheld by Congress, but they are held up for scrutiny by performers at the Woolly Mammoth, DC's edgy theater company, established in 1978 by two young New York actors. Goodnight Desdemona and The Rocky Horror Show have both graced the stage here, alongside up-and-coming plays from new

writers. In May 2005, after more than four years of performing in other venues, Woolly Mammoth opened the doors of its first permanent home — a new 265-seat, courtyard-style theatre

The Studio Theatre

1501 14th Street, NW, 202-232-7267. Box office: 202-332-3300. www.studiotheatre.org.

Dedicated to showcasing the work of contemporary playwrights, Arena Stage puts on an eclectic mix of productions ranging from the serious to the sublime. August Wilson, Neil LaBute and Eve Ensler have all had works performed at Arena. In 1988, The Studio Theatre's 2nd stage, located upstairs, opened as a place for emerging and established local and national artists to share their talents. The 2nd stage's recent production of Jerry Springer: The Opera packed the house.

Capitol Steps

Fri & Sat nights at the Ronald Reagan Building & International Trade Center, 1300 Pennsylvania Ave. NW. 202-397-7328. www.capsteps.com.

Just in case you thought Capitol Hill was all about political correctness, this two-hour comedy show will have you rolling in the aisles. Billed as "musical political satire" and performed by current and former congressional staffers, the Capitol Steps evolved from an office Christmas party skit in 1981. These popular political satirists have kept audiences (including several presidents) roaring with their irreverent spoofs of Washington politics. Musical parodies such as "We Arm the World," "Between Iraq and a Hard Place," and "Fools on the Hill" make for unforgettable fun.

SHOPPING

Save room in your suitcase: Washington, DC is a wonderful place to pick up a few things you really don't need and a few you really want. Trendy boutiques and galleries punctuate the city's neighborhoods, while immense suburban malls and outlet centers are just a drive away.

Georgetown★★

Wisconsin & M Sts. NW.
www.georgetowndc.com.

Washington, DC's best-known shopping district features upscale retailers like Betsey Johnson and Swedish retailer H&M along with standbys like Gap and Banana Republic. Unique specialty stores include accessory haven **Hats in the Belfry** (*1237 Wisconsin Ave. NW; 202-342-2006; www.hatsinthe belfry.com*), and **Commander Salamander** (*3225 M St. NW*), which is everything punk. The four-level Victorian Mall, **Georgetown Park** (*3222 M St. NW; 202-298-5577*), features an irresistible mix of upscale stores and fine-art galleries. In recent years a slew of new upscale stores including Barney's CO-OP, Coach and Ralph Lauren Rugby have set up shop along Georgetown's picturesque streets. Along the way stop at **Dean & DeLuca's** (*3276 M Street NW*) espresso bar for a caffeine break and to browse the store's selection of gourmet foods and gifts. **Ching Ching CHA House of Tea** sells an extensive selection of teawares and Asian handicrafts in the small shop in front of the tea house.

Sisters Sophie LaMontagne and Katherine Kallinis sell little bites of heaven in almost two dozen flavors at **Georgetown Cupcake** (*1209 Potomac St NW*). Be prepared to wait in line for these wildly popular sweets and be prepared to admit it was worth the wait. For a decidedly healthier treat, head up to the corner of 26th and O Streets where local farmers sell fresh produce Wednesday from 4pm–7pm (mid-May–Oct 31).

Union Station★

50 Massachusetts Ave. NE.
202-289-1908. www.union
stationdc.com.

You don't need to plan a train trip to experience DC's glorious Union Station. Designed by Daniel Burnham, the magnificently refurbished 1907 Beaux-Arts building now houses one of the District's most popular shopping and dining complexes. Familiar retailers such as **The Body Shop** and **Ann Taylor** join specialty shops, a food

---

To Market, To Market

Don't overlook DC's neighborhood markets. At **Eastern Market** (*7th St. & North Carolina Ave. S.E.; www.easternmarket.net*) on Capitol Hill, locals sift through fresh produce, baked goods, and succulent meats and cheeses. On Sundays, **Georgetown Flea Market** (*Wisconsin Ave., between S & T Sts. NW; www.georgetownfleamarket.com*) stocks an unbeatable selection of home furnishings, political memorabilia and vintage clothing.

MUST DO

Union Station

court and fine restaurants here beneath the breathtaking barrel-vaulted ceiling. **Appalachian Spring**, a local store devoted to selling American crafts, has one of its five area stores in the East Hall and the staff here are experts in packing delicate wares for travel.

Museum Gift Shops

Psst, here's a Washingtonian shopping secret—museum gift shops. You can find some truly unique items in the shops at these and other DC museums:

National Building Museum *(401 F St.; 202-272-2448; www.nbm.org)* is the place to find ergonomic office supplies and a refreshingly original selection of gifts like nut and bolt salt and peppers shakers, slang flashcards and buildings of the world Christmas ornaments.

International Spy Museum *(800 F St. NW; 202-393-7798; www.spy museum.org)* stocks spy gadgets and disguises. **National Gallery of Art** *(Madison Dr., (between 3rd & 7th Sts. NW; 202-737-4215; www. nga.gov)* features museum-inspired jewelry, scarves, prints and notecards that make great gifts.

The Textile Museum Shop *(2320 S Street, NW; 202-667-0441, www. textilemuseumshop.com)* this little gem of a museum houses a little gem of a gift shop stocked with exquisite handstitched items from around the world.

At the **Smithsonian Institution** *(on the Mall; 202-357-2700; www.si.edu; see Museums)*, you can buy everything from Astronaut ice cream (Air & Space) and presidential-campaign memorabilia (American History) to gemstones and dinosaur-assembly kits (Natural History).

Literary DC

It's no surprise that the city that packs the country's greatest concentration of PhDs also offers an impressive array of bookstores. Some of the best include **Kramerbooks and Afterwards Café** *(1517 Connecticut Ave. NW; 202-387-1400)*, on Dupont Circle; and **Politics & Prose Bookstore** *(5015 Connecticut Ave. NW; 202-364-1919)*, known for its savvy, outspoken clientele and author talks.

SHOPPING

97

Bargain Hunting

Looking for a good deal? The DC metropolitan area is surrounded by outlet malls. The largest, **Potomac Mills** boasts more than 220 discount stores *(25mi south of DC in Prince William, VA; take I-95 South to Exit 158B/Prince William Pkwy.; 703-496-9355; www.millscorp.com).* Maryland's **Arundel Mills** is home to more than 200 retailers, as well as a 24-screen movieplex *(27mi north of DC in Hanover, MD; take I-295 North to Arundel Mills Blvd.; 410-540-5110; www.millscorp.com).*

U Street

14th & U Sts. NW.

Head to the revitalized U Street neighborhood for a crash course in home décor. Poking fun at the city's quest for statehood, **Home Rule** *(1807 14th St., NW; 202-797-5544)* is where you shop for a shower curtain that resembles bubble wrap, or a toilet plunger shaped like an Academy Award. Next door, **Go Mama Go!** *(1809 14th St. NW; 202-299-0850)* packs goodies from an international bazaar into an urban storefront. Or let your shopping odyssey take you a block over and back in time to **Millennium Decorative Arts** *(1528 U St. NW; 202-483-1218)* for mid-century housewares, clothing, and knickknacks.

Fashionistas will want to melt some plastic at **Moojoo Ken** *(1512 U Street, NW; 202-234-3140)*, a tiny luxury store tucked away in a row house on U Street. The cozy boutique sells an eclectic line of funky handbags, shoes and boots that take their names from Washington, DC neighborhoods, streets, and sites. Pop into **Redeem** *(1734 14th St. NW; 202-332-7447)* or **Nana** *(1528 U St. NW; 202-667-6955),* to find the perfect outfit to go with those perfect new shoes and handbag.

It would be a crime against your sweet tooth to come to U Street and not stop by **Cakelove** *(1506 U St.)* or the **Love Café** *(across the street at 1501 U St., NW).* The bakery has something of a cult following here in town and its lawyer-turned-master-baker founder has even been featured on The Oprah Winfrey Show. Don't forget to check out the café's make-your-own cupcake bar.

Suburban Malls

Located in nearby Arlington, Virginia, **Fashion Centre at Pentagon City** features 160 stores, and it's linked to DC via the Metrorail system *(4mi south of DC, 1100 S. Hayes St.; take I-395 South to Exit 8/Washington Blvd./Ridge Rd.; 703-415-2400; www.fashioncentre pentagon.com).*

Tysons Corner Center claims more than 250 stores, with anchors Nordstrom, Bloomingdales and Lord & Taylor *(off I-495 on Rte. 7; 1961 Chain Bridge Rd., McLean,*

U Street Market

U Street, like many DC neighborhoods, hosts a weekly farmer's market. The sidewalk market at 14th and U Streets., NW, *(in front of the Reeves Center)*, sells fresh dairy, meats and produce from local farmers and runs rain or shine every Saturday from 9am–1pm May–Nov. You can also find baked goods and fresh flowers here.

VA; 703-893-9400; www.shoptysons. com). Just across Chain Bridge Road, the three-level **Galleria at Tysons II** *(2001 International Dr.; 703-827-7700; www.tysonsgalleria. com)* offers upscale shopping in Neiman Marcus, Saks Fifth Avenue and more than 100 specialty stores.

Penn Quarter

North of Pennsylvania Ave, between Fifth and 12th streets, NW, with 7th Street as the main drag. http://pqliving.com.

Contemporary art galleries have made a happy home in Penn Quarter, which at this point is DC's more up than coming downtown neighborhood.
Zenith Gallery *(413 7th Street NW; 202-783-2963)* has been part of the city's art scene since 1978 and showcases the work of many emerging artists. Nearby **Touch- stone Gallery** *(406 7th St NW, 202-347-2787)* is an artist-owned exhibition space that has also been around since the mid-70s. Newer players on the gallery scene also worth checking out include **Civilian Art Projects** *(406 7th Street NW, 3rd floor; 202- 347-0022)* and **Reyes + Davis Independent Exhibitions** *(923 F Street, NW, #302;202.255.5050)*. Set up like an actual apartment, a walk though **Apartment Zero** *(406 7th Street NW; 202-628-4067)* might make you want to get rid of every- thing you have at home and start over again with the super sleek furniture and fabulously modern housewares found here.
A visit to the tasting bar at **Cow- girl Creamery** *(919 F Street NW; 202.393.6880)* is another must.

Upper Northwest

The stretch of Connecticut Avenue, NW, that runs between Calvert St NW, up until Chevy Chase Circle.

Although less trendy than U Street or Penn Quarter, this pretty part of town houses its fair share of independent shops and markets. For the requisite DC souve- nirs—t-shirts, snow globes and Washington Monument pencil sharpeners—try the couple of souvenir shops (the names tend to change quickly but there always seem to be one or two) near the Woodley Park Metro stop and the tables set up across the street from the National Zoo. Cleveland Park's **Wake Up Little Susie** *(3409 Connecticut Ave, NW; 202-244-0700)* sells whimsical gifts, ceramics and jewelry, and always has a few cynical political items like onsies that say "I'm already smarter than the president."
A few doors down organic market **Yes! Natural Gourmet** *(3425 Conn. Ave, NW; 363-1559)* packs a lot into a small space.
Neighbors love **Firehook Bakery and Coffee House** *(3411 Conn. Ave, NW; 202-362-2253)* for its scrumptious cookies and for the surprisingly large and peaceful garden seating area out back. Near the circle, try **Periwinkle** *(3815 Livingston St NW; 202-364- 3076)* for fun gifts and hand painted chocolates, **Catch Can** *(5516 Conn. Ave NW; 202-686-5316)* for natural fiber clothes and comfy shoes and **Barston's Child's Play** *(5536 Connecticut Ave, NW; (202) 244-3602)* for one of the best toy stores in town.

NIGHTLIFE

Although it's largely populated by stodgy politicians, pugnacious lobbyists, and more lawyers than you can shake a stick at, DC does like to let its hair down now and then. Whether they're boogying or listening to blues music, Washingtonians love their nightlife. Here's where the cognoscenti head after all those boring receptions on the Hill.

The Black Cat

1811 14th St. NW, U St. area. 202-667-7960. www.blackcatdc.com.

Music lovers flock to The Black Cat for a sneak preview of some of rock's rising stars. The club runs two stages. The larger Mainstage plays host to national independent touring acts and underground/alternative acts. Downstairs the smaller Backstage is a more intimate performance space, showcasing indie, punk and garage rock bands. Backstage also holds monthly DJ dance nights. If you want something more low-key (or just don't feel like emptying your pockets to pay the cover charge) check out the club's no-cover Red Room Bar, also downstairs. The familiar U Street haunt is co-owned by former Nirvana drummer and current Foo Fighter Dave Grohl.

What's Up?

For the latest on who's playing where, consult the Friday Weekend section of the *Washington Post,* or check the entertainment pages online at www.washington post.com.

Blues Alley

1073 Wisconsin Ave. NW, Georgetown. 202-337-4141. www.bluesalley.com.

Few Washington clubs have enjoyed the success and notoriety of Georgetown's Blues Alley, which has been praised by no less than Dizzy Gillespie. Some of the biggest names in jazz have played and recorded albums in the venerable venue, tucked away in a Georgetown alley.

The Black Cat

Bryan Whitson/The Black Cat

Hotel Hot Spots

Some of the hottest spots in town are housed in Washington's hip new hotels. Sex and attitude permeate the menu of adventurous drinks at **Bar Rouge** *(1315 16th St. NW; 202-232-8000; www.rougehotel.com)* at the Hotel Rouge. Choose a sultry Femme Fatale or Sin on the Rocks. At the Hotel Helix, the retro **Helix Lounge** *(1430 Rhode Island Ave. NW; 202-234-1454; www.hotelhelix.com)* serves Pabst Blue Ribbon beer in a room drenched in white vinyl.

Bohemian Caverns

2001 11th St. NW, U St. Area. 202-299-0801. www.bohemian caverns.com.

Back in the day, jazz legends like Billie Holiday, Count Basie, Sarah Vaugn, Duke Ellington, Charlie Parker, Billy Eckstein, and John Coltrane would come perform here after they finished their gigs at all-white establishments. The new Bohemian Caverns recently reopened with a fresh look and a new lineup of performers. An upscale restaurant occupies the upper level, while live music trickles up from the caverns below.

The Brickskeller

1523 22nd St NW, Dupont Circle. 202-293-1885. www.lovethe beer.com.

If you've never met a beer you didn't like, you'll make a lot of friends at The Brickskeller. The pub, which has been serving up cold ones to Washingtonians since 1957, offers a selection of hundreds of beers from around the world including brews from Venezuela, Japan and Latvia. The staff here prides themselves on finding new beers to serve and is good at making recommendations. The Brickskeller also has a full menu and runs a 42-room, boarding-house style hotel above the saloon.

Eighteenth Street Lounge

1212 18th St. NW, Adams Morgan. 202-466-3922. www.eslmusic.com.

Celebrity residents and visitors are often spotted in ESL (as it's known to locals), one of Adams Morgan's hippest nightlife spots. Bouncers guard the beautiful property—a historic mansion that was once home to Teddy Roosevelt—and maintain a strict admissions policy that leaves many on the front side of the door. (You must dress to impress to have a shot at getting in—no jeans, sneakers or khakis.) The strict dress code coupled with the fact that there is no sign outside announcing the club, are the first clues that ESL truly is a place to see and be seen.

Enology

3238 Wisconsin Avenue, NW, Cleveland Park. 202-362-0362. www.enologydc.com.

Red, white and blue rules the menu at Enology wine bar. (Hey, this is the nation's capital, after all.) All the wine, beer, liquor and food served here are produced in the United States. Even the playlist is courtesy of artists from the nifty 50. Enology is a good choice if you want to have a lovely evening with a few friends or that one special one. Clean modern lines,

NIGHTLIFE

subtle tones and low lighting helps create the perfect ambiance for a night of unwinding while sampling good domestic wines, cheeses and chocolates.

HR-57

1610 Fourteenth Street NW, U Street. 202-667-3700. www.hr57.org.

A musical cultural center, HR-57 Center takes its name from a House Resolution passed by Congress in 1987 which designated jazz as "a rare and valuable national American treasure". Here aspiring musicians and world-renowned artists perform jazz and blues. The HR-57 Foundation, which sponsors the performance space, helps bring music to the city's schools and universities.

Irelands Four Fields

3412 Connecticut Ave NW, Cleveland Park. (202)244-0860. www.irelandsfourprovinces.com/

This is one of those neighborhood bars where everyone knows your name, so it seems only fair that you should know that despite the sign outside everyone in town refers to this establishment as the 4Ps (From back when it was called the Four Providences). A favorite among locals, this Irish pub serves food and beer into the night and sometimes has live music. The Wednesday trivia night has found something of a cult following among Washington know-it-alls and this is "the" place to be on St. Patrick's Day.

Local 16

1602 U St NW, U Street. (202) 265-2828. www.tablezen.com/local16.

During summer weeknights the outdoor deck of Local 16's Italian Renaissance style lounge is a great spot to unwind with a cocktail in hand and friends at your side. The popular deck is opened 9 months out of the year and on chillier evenings staff set up portable heaters. Along with the bar, there are a few tables outside and you can order off the menu used inside. Fridays and Saturdays the mood goes from laid back to high-energy when the house DJ starts spinning at 10pm.

Madam's Organ

2461 18th St. NW, Adams Morgan. 202-667-5370. www.madams organ.com.

"Sorry, we're open" reads the mural outside, just below a busty redhead's boldly painted portrait. The bright colors and brazen sarcasm of Madam's Organ have made it one of the most familiar sites in DC. Inside, it's just as quirky. Take the stairs up to Big Daddy's Love Lounge & Pick-Up Joint, but beware—it's aptly named. If you are still awake, Madam's Organ serves brunch on the weekends from 12pm–4pm.

MCCXXIII

1223 Connecticut Ave. NW, Dupont Circle. 202-822-1800. www.1223.com.

Billing itself as Washington's "Premier Champagne and Caviar Club," this is a place for those who take nightlife seriously. MCCXXIII wards

MUST DO

off the not-so-chic Dupont Circle denizens from its classy clientele.

Nightclub 9:30

815 V St. NW, at 9th St. & Vermont Ave., U St. area. 202-265-0930. www.930.com.

This storied club can pack in 1,200 people to listen to an enticing lineup of local and national acts. The edgy 9:30 Club (as it is known locally) attracts a young crowd ("all ages, all the time") who don't mind that the club is standing-room only—there are no seats but there are four bars to help you take your mind off your feet.

The Rock and Roll Hotel

1353 H Street, NE, H Street Corridor. 202-388-7625. www.rockandroll hoteldc.com.

Washington's music scene crowds the Rock and Roll Hotel for its live edgy music on the ground floor and theme rooms upstairs. The theme rooms (featuring various options such as a digital jukebox, piano, bar and pool table) can be rented for the night but are not for overnights, despite the hotel in the club's name. The owners created the venue as a homage to hotels like the Savoy in London and The Chelsea in New York City.

Third Edition

1218 Wisconsin Ave. NW, Georgetown. 202-333-3700. www.thethirdedition.com.

This Georgetown mainstay served as the backdrop for the movie St. Elmo's Fire and has hosted many a college student since it opened in 1969. On Wednesday through Saturday nights, a dance party erupts on the upper level, leaving the mellow downstairs beer-sippers in the wake of rock classics. In the summertime, the lively Tiki Bar offers one of Georgetown's few opportunities for outdoor nightlife off the riverfront.

The Wonderland Ballroom

1101 Kenyon St, NW, Columbia Heights. 202-232-5263. www. thewonderlandballroom.com.

A self-described bohemian beer garden, The Wonderland Ballroom is two floors of beer, live music and hang out space. Among the bar food the kitchen serves up are burgers, dogs, sausages and Chilli – and vegetarian versions of them all. Monday trivia night attracts a large and sometimes cut throat crowd. Anyone can sign up to write questions or play and $3 bottles of beer flow freely.

Rock and Roll Hotel

Rock and Roll Hotel

SPAS

Even Washington, DC's biggest egos need to be massaged once in a while. Tired tourists and power players alike can find refuge in a pedicure or facial at the many day spas in the nation's capital. From downtown to Georgetown, there's no shortage of spas that cater to the hard-working politicos, social activists and soccer moms of the Washington, DC metropolitan area.

Andre Chreky

1604 K St. NW. 202-293-9393. www.andrechreky.com.

One of Washington's most revered hair salons doubles as a day spa, where you can pop in for a quick manicure or melt into a relaxing massage. Located in the bustling business district, it's a popular stop for hardworking lawyers and lobbyists. Indulge in complimentary pastries and cappuccinos while you await your treatment. Most body and face treatments here run about $100.

Bluemercury

Bluemercury

3059 M St. NW. 202-965-1300. 1619 Connecticut Ave. NW. 202-462-1300. www.bluemercury.com.

This Washington and New York-based purveyor of upscale beauty products gets rave reviews for its pain-free waxing and high-tech oxygen facials. With locations in Georgetown and Dupont Circle, the spa draws a young, fashion-conscious crowd for its stylish treatments and funky cosmetics. For an extra healthy glow, add an eye-zone treatment, glycolic peel, microdermabrasion, vitamin oxygen blast, or a vitamin C treatment to any traditional facial. It's a bit on the pricey side, but, hey, you're worth it.

Capital City Club and Spa

1001 16th St. NW. 202-639-4300. www.capitalcityspa.com.

Housed in the Capital Hilton, the Capital City Club and Spa is a popular 11,000-square-foot workout facility that offers an array of spa packages and treatment options. After an invigorating workout, treat yourself to a Reiki healing session or a deep-tissue massage. Instead of that 5pm martini, try the "Happy Hour Alternative," featuring an hour-long massage, a therapeutic facial, and a spa manicure and pedicure.

MUST DO

Celadon

1180 F St. NW. 202-347-3333. www.celadonspa.com.

Hot-stone massages and anti-aging manicures beckon at this oasis, nestled among downtown office buildings. Celadon's treatment rooms are washed in muted shades of green and illuminated solely by aromatherapy candles. Sugar scrubs and alpha-hydroxy facials make city life a little more bearable. Want to go more than skin deep? Celadon offers Botox, Restylan and laser treatments.

Elizabeth Arden Red Door

5225 Wisconsin Ave. NW. 202-363-1627. www.reddoorsalons.com. Additional locations in Bethesda, Arlington, Reston, Fairfax, and Vienna, Virginia.

Classic Red Door treatments are available at several locations throughout the area. A favorite choice for Washington celebrities, local brides and famous faces.

Four Seasons Fitness Club and Spa

Four Seasons Hotel, 2800 Pennsylvania Ave. NW. 202-342-0444. www.fourseasons.com.

Frequently voted best in the city, this Georgetown landmark takes a cue from the Four Seasons spa in Bali for its luxurious skin treatments and massages but adds a local twist. Your skin will never feel as smooth as after the spa's cherry blossom champagne body treatment ($225) or a Capital Hill scrub ($155) which uses ruby grapefruit and blood orange extracts.

Grooming Lounge

Grooming Lounge

The Grooming Lounge

1745 L St. NW. 202-466-8900. www.groominglounge.com.

Who said indulgence was just for women? While most of the city's spas welcome male patrons with "just for men" packages, this one takes it a step further. The Grooming Lounge is a downtown gentlemen's salon, where guys can enjoy a hot-lather shave or a business manicure. The lounge also offers assistance in tackling embarrassing problems such as back hair and unibrows.

The Sports Club/LA Splash

Ritz-Carlton Washington, 1170 22nd St. NW. 202-974-6600. www.thesportsclubla.com.

A favorite retreat for visitors and Washingtonians, showy Splash delights clients with its signature Soft Pack flotation device. Once you're unwrapped from this unique water-filled blanket, you'll find yourself blissfully limp and feeling virtually weightless. Splash is also known for its massages and offers half-day, full-day and week-long packages.

NEARBY NORTHERN VIRGINIA

Just across the river from DC, the sprawling suburbs of Northern Virginia lie within easy commuting distance of the city. That's where you'll find historic sites including George Washington's plantation and the venerable Arlington National Cemetery, as well as plentiful opportunities for recreation. You'll also find Old Town, Alexandria, a tony community that developed on land that was annexed back from the capital city in 1846.

Mount Vernon★★★

16mi south of DC in Alexandria, VA., via the George Washington Memorial Pkwy. 703-780-2000. www.mountvernon.org. Open daily Apr–Aug 8am–5pm; Mar, Sept & Oct 9am–5pm; Nov–Feb 9am–4pm. $13.

George Washington didn't tell a lie when he referred to his plantation home, which sits on a grassy slope overlooking the Potomac River, as a "well-resorted tavern."
In one year alone, the statesman received 432 visitors at Mount Vernon, where he escaped the stress of public office and enjoyed the life of a successful Virginia planter. Today Mount Vernon is still welcoming guests as America's

The Gentleman Farmer
Washington considered farming the "most delectable" occupation. *"It is honorable,"* he wrote, *"it is amusing, and, with judicious management, it is profitable."*

most-visited historic estate. Over the years Washington increased Mount Vernon's holdings to more than 8,000 acres, which were divided into five independent but adjoining farms and worked by some 300 slaves.

The Mansion
In 1858 the Mount Vernon Ladies Association raised the $200,000 necessary to buy the estate. The mansion's broad, columned piazza

Mount Vernon

Mount Vernon Ladies' Association

Mount Vernon Trail
Running alongside the George Washington Memorial Parkway, this popular paved biking and walking path leads through wetlands along the Potomac River. Turnouts, particularly south of Old Town, Alexandria, allow you to park and walk—or bike—as far as you like. Bike trail maps are available at the visitor center in Alexandria *(221 King St.; 703-838-4200; www.visitalexandriava.com).*

is Mount Vernon's hallmark. The Georgian farmhouse is set off by a rust-red roof and curved colonnades that connect the two flanking wings. A frugal man, Washington faced the house with "rusticated board," a wood siding plastered with sand to resemble white stone—which was much more expensive. The décor inside the house reflects Washington's final years there, and many of the furnishings belonged to him.

- **Central Hall** – Pine paneling here is "grained" to resemble mahogany. The hall opens onto four rooms and the piazza. From the piazza, there's a lovely view★ of the Potomac River and the distant Maryland shore.
- **Dining Room** – This lavish room, with its ornate wood-work, Palladian windows and marble mantel, was the last addition to the house.
- **Master Bedroom** – Simply furnished, Washington's room contains the mahogany four-poster bed in which he died.
- **Washington's Study** – A narrow back staircase leads down to Washington's first-floor study, which contains his desk and his presidential desk chair, and a terrestrial globe commissioned from a London manufacturer.

The Grounds

Forty acres of forests and land-scaped flower and vegetable gardens occupy the estate's grounds, along with 12 small dependencies. These structures re-create the operations of a self-sufficient estate, from the curing, spinning and laundry houses to the living quarters for overseers and slaves.

- **Burial Sites** – The tombs of George and Martha Washington lie beyond the stables. Beyond an iron grille, the couple's marble sarcophagi are visible within an open vault. Interred

NEARBY NORTHERN VIRGINIA

Mount Vernon Time Line
- **1674** – King Charles II grants the property to George's great-grandfather.
- **1740** – George's father deeds the property to his son Lawrence. Lawrence renames the 2,500-acre estate Mount Vernon, after an admiral he admired while serving in the Royal Navy.
- **1752** – When Lawrence dies, 20-year-old George takes over managing Mount Vernon.
- **1759** – Washington marries Martha Dandridge Custis, a widow with two children. To accommodate his new family, Washington redecorates and enlarges the property's simple farmhouse.
- **1799** – Washington dies in his bed at Mount Vernon.

in the walls of the vault are 27 other family members. On a hill near the Washington tomb sits the slave burial ground which today is marked by a memorial to honor the African-American slaves and free blacks who worked at Mount Vernon during the 18C and the first half of the 19C. As was typical of the time, the graves were unmarked, and the identities and numbers of those laid to rest there are largely unknown. *Slave Life at Mount Vernon* tours leave from the Mansion Circle everyday at 10am, 12pm and 2pm from Apr–Oct.

- **Pioneer Farm** – Located near the wharf, the farm features demonstrations of 18C animal husbandry, crop cultivation and brick making.

Arlington National Cemetery★★

On the Arlington side of Memorial Bridge, about ¾mi from the Lincoln Memorial. 703-607-8000. www.arlingtoncemetery.org. Open Apr–Sept daily 8am–7pm. Rest of the year daily 8am–5pm.

Touring the Cemetery
The cemetery is situated on hilly land crisscrossed with meandering paved routes. Car traffic is permitted only for disabled visitors and for relatives of persons buried here. A Tourmobile shuttle operates within the cemetery and stops at the most popular sights (Kennedy gravesites, Tomb of the Unknowns and Arlington House). Purchase tickets for the tour at the visitor center on Memorial Drive.

Endless rows of gleaming white headstones at Arlington National Cemetery may well bring a tear to your eye. The country's most revered burial ground contains the graves of more than 300,000 military personnel and their dependents. Among those laid to rest in the rolling hills of this 612-acre military cemetery are veterans of every armed conflict in which the US has participated since the Revolutionary War.

At the outbreak of the Civil War, the Union Army took Arlington House (opposite) as its Washington headquarters, and military installations were erected around the 1,100-acre estate. With much of

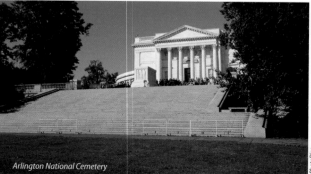

Arlington National Cemetery

©PhotoDisc

the fighting taking place around the capital, the need for burial space soon became evident. In 1864, 200 acres of the estate were designated as a burial ground and Arlington House was claimed by the federal government.

In 1883 the Lee family, who owned the land at the time, accepted a financial compensation of $150,000 from the government rather than demanding restitution for the estate, which by then contained the remains of some 16,000 war casualties. That same year, Arlington became the official cemetery of the US.

Kennedy Gravesites –

An eternal flame marks the simple grave of President John F. Kennedy (1917–1963). Nearby, the grave of John's younger brother, Robert F. Kennedy (1925–1968), is indicated by a white cross.

Tomb of the Unknowns –

Located behind the Memorial Amphitheater, this tomb contains the remains of soldiers from each of the two world wars and the Korean War. They symbolize all the men and women who lost their lives in those conflicts as well as in the Vietnam War.

Changing of the Guard – Don't miss seeing the precision and skill of the military sentries *(daily from Apr–Oct on the half-hour; rest of the year daily on the hour).*

Arlington House, The Robert E. Lee Memorial★

On the grounds of Arlington National Cemetery. 703-235-1530. www.nps.gov/arho. Open year-round daily 9:30am–4:30pm. Closed Jan 1 & Dec 25. (Arlington House is currently empty of furnishings so it can embark on a restoration project beginning in 2008 and scheduled to be completed in 2010. The house will continue to be open to the public while much of the work is conducted with some exceptions. It's best to call ahead prior to visiting.)

Surrounded by the white headstones of Arlington Cemetery, this Greek Revival-style house has known its share of famous occupants. Arlington House was built in 1818 by George Washington Parke Custis (his father, John, was the son of Martha Washington by her first husband). When John Custis died during the Revolution, George and Nelly, the youngest of his four children, were brought to

Iwo Jima Memorial★

Just outside Arlington National Cemetery via the Ord and Weitzel Gate.
This striking sculpture honors all US Marines who have lost their lives in military duty. The statue of six American soldiers raising the Stars and Stripes on Mount Suribachi represents an event that took place in 1945 during the assault on the Japanese-controlled island of Iwo Jima. The capture of this strategically located island is considered one of the Marines' greatest victories of World War II. Based on the Pulitzer Prize-winning war photograph by Joseph Rosenthal, the memorial was designed by Horace W. Peaslee and sculpted by Felix de Weldon.

Manassas National Battlefield Park

©ARSNL/Wikimedia Commons

Mount Vernon and raised by the Washingtons. After Martha Washington died in 1802, 21-year-old George Custis constructed Arlington House on a 1,100-acre tract of land his father had left him. Enter Robert E. Lee. A distant relative of the Custises, Lee grew up in nearby Alexandria, Virginia, and visited the Custis home often as a boy. In 1831 he married Mary Anna Randolph Custis, the only surviving child of George and Mary Lee, at Arlington House. At the Custises' death, title to the mansion passed to the Lees. During the Civil War, the estate grounds were turned into a national cemetery *(see p 108)* for the Civil War dead. Today the official Robert E. Lee Memorial, furnished with 19C period and Lee family pieces, commands an exceptional view★★ of DC.

Tomb of Pierre L'Enfant – On the lawn in front of Arlington House is the tomb of the man who designed the original city plan for Washington, DC.

Manassas National Battlefield Park★★

29mi southwest of DC in Manassas, VA. Take I-66 West to Exit 47B (Rte. 234 North). Go through the first traffic light, and the visitor center will be on the right at 6411 Sudley Rd. 703-361-1339. www.nps. gov/mana. Open year-round daily from dawn until dusk. $3. Visitor center opened daily 8:30pm–5pm and closed Thanksgiving Day & Dec 25.

When you see these peaceful fields now, it's hard to imagine the brutal battles that were fought on this ground. In fact, the first major land battle of the Civil War took place here on Henry Hill, overlooking a creek call Bull Run.
On the morning of July 21, 1861, the 35,000-man Union Army set out from the capital city under the command of General Irvin McDowell to confront the Confederates at Manassas, a key railroad junction southwest of DC. The men, mostly 90-day volunteers, were feeling cocky; they were sure the Rebels would turn tail at the first shot. And a victory here would pave the way to a march

As things were looking grim for the Confederate Army early in the first Battle of Bull Run, commander Barnard Bee tried to keep the Confederate lines from collapsing. Seeing newly arrived general Thomas J. Jackson sitting tall in the saddle alongside his brigade, Bee shouted: "There stands Jackson like a stone wall! Rally behind the Virginians!"

on Richmond, the Confederate capital, and a quick end to the war. Confidence was so high that DC residents even packed picnic lunches and rode out to enjoy the show. But the show they saw was not what they expected. The plucky Confederates stayed to fight, and the violence that followed shocked spectators and soldiers alike. At first the Union forces had the upper hand, but as Confederate reinforcements arrived, the battle's momentum began to shift. By the end of the day, the Confederates had pushed the Federals back across Bull Run, and McDowell's exhausted troops began to retreat.

An important Confederate victory, the First Battle of Bull Run—with its death toll of 900 young men— also proved to everyone that the war would not end quickly. Indeed, the two armies clashed again thirteen months later on the same ground. This time the Union suffered an even greater defeat, at the hands of General Robert E. Lee.

Henry Hill Visitor Center – Houses a museum with displays that set the stage and describe the battle. Here you can see the film, Manassas: End of Innocence.

Walking Tours – Choose from a 1mi loop of Henry Hill, or two 5mi loops covering the battle grounds of the first (1861) and second (1862) battles at Manassas.

Driving Tour – This 13mi, self-guided drive covers 11 key sites of the second battle at Bull Run.

Old Town, Alexandria★★

8mi south of DC via the George Washington Memorial Pkwy. Ramsey House Visitor Center is located at 221 King St. 703-838-4200 or 800-388-9119. Open daily 9am–8pm. Closed Thanksgiving Day, Dec 25, and Jan 1. www.funside.com.

When you tire of the hustle and bustle of the city, hop on the Metro (get off at King St.) and spend a day in Old Town. This walkable, tree-shaded enclave of brick sidewalks, shops, restaurants and 18C architecture on the banks

Brigitta L. House/Michelin

Old Town, Alexandria

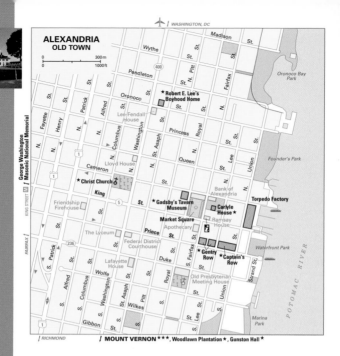

ALEXANDRIA
OLD TOWN

Madison St.
Wythe St.
Pendleton St.
Oronoco St.
★ Robert E. Lee's Boyhood Home
Lee-Fendall House
Princess St.
Queen St.
Lloyd House
Cameron St.
★ Christ Church
King St.
Friendship Firehouse
★ Gadsby's Tavern Museum
Carlyle House ★
Market Square
Ramsay House
Apothecary
The Lyceum
Prince St.
Federal District Courthouse
Lafayette House
Duke St.
Wolfe St.
Old Presbyterian Meeting House
Wilkes St.
Gibbon St.

George Washington Masonic National Memorial
KING STREET
FAIRFAX

Oronoco Bay Park
Founder's Park
Bank of Alexandria
Torpedo Factory
Waterfront Park
POTOMAC RIVER
Marina Park

300 m
1000 ft

/ RICHMOND

/ MOUNT VERNON ★★★, Woodlawn Plantation ★, Gunston Hall ★

of the Potomac River just oozes Colonial charm and slow-paced Southern gentility.

The area now called Old Town, Alexandria, began with a tobacco warehouse built on the waterfront in the early 1700s. Prominent Scottish tobacco merchants and Virginia tobacco planters petitioned the Virginia General Assembly to establish a town here, and in 1748 the government granted their request. The 60-acre tract on which the town was to be sited belonged to members of the Alexander family, and thus the new town was named Alexandria.

In its early years, Alexandria flourished as a lively colonial seaport. It was a mixture of warehouses, shipyards, taverns, small clapboard dwellings and fine Georgian mansions, like Carlyle House★, home of Scottish immigrant John Carlyle *(121 N. Fairfax St.; 703-549-2997; www.carlylehouse.org)*. During the Revolution, Alexandria was a meeting place for such leaders

Torpedo Factory

105 N. Union St. 703-838-4565. www.torpedofactory.org.

Art fans won't want to miss Alexandria's extensive visual-arts center. Overlooking the Potomac River, the cavernous building was indeed used to manufacture topedoes during the world wars. Now it houses the studios and shops of more than 150 professional artists and craftspeople.

MUST SEE

George Washington Masonic National Memorial

101 Callahan Dr. at the west end of King St. 703-683-2007. www.gwmemorial.org. Open year-round daily 9am–4pm. Closed Jan 1, Dec 25 & federal holidays.
This memorial to George Washington, the first master of Alexandria's Masonic Lodge, anchors the west end of Old Town. The large granite building, topped by a seven-story tiered tower, is modeled after the lighthouse on the island of Pharos near Alexandria, Egypt. Begun in 1923, the memorial was built in increments over the course of 40 years.

as George Mason, who lived at nearby Gunston Hall, and George Washington, whose plantation, Mount Vernon, was located 8mi down the Potomac. At the height of the war, in 1779, Alexandria was incorporated as a town.

A Day in Old Town

- Stroll along brick-paved **Gentry Row★** *(200 block of Prince St.)* and cobblestone **Captain's Row★** *(100 block of Prince St.),* where 18C and 19C town houses recall Alexandria's seafaring days.
- Sample colonial fare at 1770 **Gadsby's Tavern Museum★**, considered in its day to be the finest public house in the new capital *(134 N. Royal St.; museum visit by guided tour only; restaurant open to the public; 703-838-4242; www.gadsbystavern.org).*
- Browse the shops along **King Street,** Old Town's main commercial thoroughfare. Along the way you'll pass **Market Square** *(between Royal & Fairfax Sts.),* dominated by the steepled 1873 City Hall.
- Visit venerable **Christ Church★** *(corner of N. Washington & Cameron Sts.; 703-549-1450).* Both George Washington and Robert E. Lee worshipped in the simple brick and stone 1773 structure. By tradition, 20C pres-

idents worship in Washington's pew on the Sunday nearest his birthday (February 22).
- Walk by **Robert E. Lee's Boyhood Home★** *(607 Oronoco St.; closed to the public),* where Lee lived when he was young.

Great Falls Park★

15mi north of DC in McLean, VA. Take the George Washington Memorial Pkwy. North to the exit for I-495 South. Exit on Rte. 193 (Georgetown Pike) and turn right on Old Dominion Dr. Follow Old Dominion about 4.5mi and turn right at sign for Great Falls. 703-285-2965. www.nps.gov/gwmp/grfa. Open year round daily 7am–dusk. $5 per vehicle. Closed Dec 25.

Great Falls may not be a theme-park ride, but it is an awesome series of cascading rapids that drop 76 feet in elevation over a distance of less than a mile. Here the waters of the Potomac River gather speed as they narrow from 2,500 feet to 60 feet and funnel through the jagged cliffs of Mather Gorge. First identified by an early settler as the "Great Falls of the Potomac," the falls were the site of an amusement park in the early 1900s. The park was a huge success until floods damaged its structures. Rejected by the Potomac Power Company as unfit

Great Falls Park Historic Site

©La Wanda Wilson/Dreamstime.com

for hydroelectric development, the land came into the hands of the National Park Service in 1966. Today the 800-acre park, with its series of 20-foot-high falls, provides visitors with a spectacular setting in which to hike, bike, horseback ride, picnic or just enjoy the view. Drink in as much of the breathtaking scenery as you want but please remember to put safety first. Swimming and wading in the Potomac is dangerous and absolutely forbidden at Great Falls.

River Trail – Begins just downstream of the falls and leads along the clifftops for 3mi *(allow 2hrs)*, allowing fantastic views of the roaring whitewater.

Patowmack Canal Trail – This 2.5mi trail *(allow 1hr)* passes ruins of the Patowmack Canal, now a Civil Engineering Landmark, en route to the head of the falls.

Gunston Hall★

20mi south of DC. Take I-95 South to Exit 163, then follow the signs to Gunston Hall. From Mount Vernon or Woodlawn, continue south on US-1 and turn left on Gunston Rd. (Rte. 242.) 703-550-9220. www.gunstonhall.org. Open year-round daily 9:30am–5pm.

The Patowmack Canal

George Washington's pet project, the Patowmack Canal was intended to connect the East Coast with the head-waters of the Ohio River, thereby opening a waterway west for trade. In 1784 the Patowmack Company was established to build a canal with a series of locks that would make the Potomac River navigable between Georgetown and the river's headwaters at Cumberland, Maryland. Crews began work in 1786, but roaring rapids, solid rock and plunging falls slowed their progress and the canal took 16 years to complete. Unfortunately, Washington died in 1799, two years before the canal opened at Great Falls. Although the waterway operated for more than 20 years, in the end the venture was a failure. High construction costs bankrupted the Patowmack Company in 1828, and the canal was eventually abandoned.

MUST SEE

Guided tours given every half-hour. Closed Jan 1, Thanksgiving Day & Dec 25. $8.

Sure you've heard of George Washington and Thomas Jefferson, but how about George Mason? If you've read the Constitution of the United States, you've read his words (see sidebar below). Now a relatively obscure patriot, George Mason (1725–1792) in his day was a respected thinker whose writings influenced the course of the Revolution and the development of the young Republic.

In 1755 Mason began constructing his Georgian manor house on the Virginia shoreline about a mile above the Potomac—not far from Mount Vernon.

With its large symmetrical chimneys and plain brick facade, Gunston Hall reflects the style of plantation life favored by wealthy 18C Virginia planters.

As young men, Mason and George Washington became friends, and over the years they frequently exchanged views about the development of the new nation. Though he served as a member of the Virginia House of Burgesses

Let Freedom Ring

"That all men are born equally free and independent and have certain inherent natural Rights… among which are the Enjoyment of Life and Liberty, with the Means of acquiring and possessing Property, and pursuing and obtaining Happiness and Safety." Sound familiar? It should. These words from the first draft of the Virginia Declaration of Rights were penned by George Mason in May 1776. Mason's friend Thomas Jefferson echoed this passage in his draft of the Declaration of Independence (July 1776).

and a delegate to the Constitutional Convention of 1787, Mason preferred to exercise his influence quietly, through writings and private conversations.

He died at Gunston Hall in 1792, just as the young Republic was being formed. Two raised sarcophagi on the estate grounds contain the remains of George Mason and his wife, Ann.

Guston Hall sponsors a full calendar of activities from open hearth cooking classes to a plantation Christmas dinner. Check the web site for details.

Virginia Tourism Corporation

Gunston Hall

NEARBY NORTHERN VIRGINIA

Pope-Leighey House

On the grounds of Woodlawn, below the parking lot. 703-780-4000. Same hours as Woodlawn. The claim to fame of this small, L-shaped house is that it was designed by renowned 20C architect Frank Lloyd Wright. Built in 1941, the 1,200-square-foot, five-room house cost roughly $7,000. Now owned by the National Trust for Historic Preservation, which moved the structure to Woodlawn, the residence contains the furniture that Wright designed for it. Only cypress, brick, glass and concrete were used to build the house, according to Wright's practice of using as few materials as possible.

What's Inside the Mansion?

- The interior of the house is noted for its mid-18C carved **woodwork** by English craftsman William Buckland.
- The **Chinese formal parlor** is the only surviving room in America featuring the scalloped Chinoiserie woodworking of the colonial period.
- English Palladian-style woodwork decorates the **dining room.**

Woodlawn★

19mi south of DC. Take the George Washington Memorial Pkwy. south to Rte. 235 South to Rte. 1 South. 9000 Richmond Hwy. (Rte. 1), Alexandria, VA. 703-780-4000.

www.woodlawn1805.org. Visit by guided tour only Mar–Dec Tue–Sun 10am–5pm. Closed Thanksgiving Day & Dec 25. $7.50; combination ticket with Pope-Leighey House $13.

It's good to have relatives in high places. That was certainly the case for Lawrence Lewis and Eleanor "Nelly" Custis Lewis, favored relatives of President George Washington and his wife, Martha (Lawrence was George's nephew; Nelly was Martha's granddaughter).
As a wedding gift, Washington gave the couple a 2,000-acre tract west of Mount Vernon. He also deeded them a nearby mill and distillery, because, as he advised Lawrence, "a young man should

West Front, Woodlawn

National Trust for Historic Preservation

have objects of employment. Idleness is disreputable." In 1802 the Lewises moved into the completed north wing of the house. After Lawrence died in 1839, Nelly went to live with her son in Clark County. Seven years later, the family offered Woodlawn at public sale. The estate knew several different owners before it became the property of the National Trust for Historic Preservation in 1957.

The Mansion – Designed by prominent architect Dr. William Thornton, this Georgian brick mansion incorporates two symmetrical one-and-a-half-story wings connected to the main house by one-story covered walkways known as "hyphens." Inside, the house contains many of the furnishings that belonged to the family, including several pieces brought over from Mount Vernon.

Prince William Forest

Prince William County, 35mi south of DC. Take I-95 south to exit 150-B (VA Route 619/Joplin Road). Park entrance is the second. 703-221-7181. www.nps.gov/prwi. Open dawn to dusk. Registered overnight campers have 24-hour access. Walk-in $3, vehicles $5 (valid for 7 days).

The Great Depression loomed over the country as President Franklin D. Roosevelt took the oath of office in 1933. Among the many efforts he initiated to pull the nation out from its crippling economic crisis were the Civilian Conservation Corps (CCC) and the Works Progress Administration (WPA), which put people to work building the country's national, state and metropolitan parks.

Through these innovative federal work programs Americans got desperately needed jobs and the country got a park system. Prince William Forest Park, originally called the Chopawamsic Recreational Development Area when created in 1934, is one of these parks. Prince William Forest Park offers visitors 37 miles of hiking trails, 21 miles of bicycle paths and overnight camping facilities. Prince William Forest Park also houses the largest inventory of CCC structures in the National Park System.

National Park Service

Prince William Forest

117

EXCURSIONS

Tired of trekking to museums and monuments in the nation's capital? Within two and a half hours, you can drive away from the city to nearby Virginia, West Virginia and Maryland. Each of these areas has its own charms, whether you prefer to delve into the history of Harpers Ferry or Colonial Williamsburg, go bird-watching on Maryland's Eastern Shore, or take a scenic drive along the Blue Ridge Parkway.

Governor's Palace, Colonial Williamsburg

©The Colonial Williamsburg Foundation

Colonial Williamsburg★★★

151mi southeast of DC via I-95 South to I-64 East. 800-447-8679. www.colonialwilliamsburg.org. Open year-round daily 9am–5pm. Hours vary at certain buildings & tradeshops. $49.

You'll think you've landed back in the 18C as you walk the streets of this painstakingly re-created 301-acre town site. Here you'll encounter costumed guides and character interpreters depicting citizens of Virginia's 18C colonial capital going about their daily routines. Just don't expect these well-versed actors to break character—they're firmly entrenched in the 18C.

Williamsburg's roots date to 1699, when colonial legislators decided to move their capital from Jamestown inland to Middle Plantation, where the **College of William**

Tips For Visiting

The best way to decipher Williamsburg is to begin at the Visitor Center *(Lafayette St. near the intersection with the Colonial Pkwy.)*, where you can purchase several different types of passes that encompass varying amounts of time and numbers of sights. Many buildings, including the Capitol and Governor's Palace, are open by guided tour only. Historic homes are open on different days of the week; check when you buy your ticket. Before you start exploring, get a grounding in the town's history by watching the 35-minute film, *Williamsburg: The Story of a Patriot.*

Colonial Williamsburg After Hours

After the crowds have left, nighttime is one of the best times to experience Colonial Williamsburg. More than 27 houses and taverns here have overnight guest rooms for rent *(800-447-8679)*. All are decorated with reproduction antiques and offer the ambience of the past with the comforts of the present. Be sure to have dinner *(reserve well in advance; 800-251-2811)* at one of the four colonial taverns—King's Arms, Christiana Campbell's, Shields, Josiah Chowning's—where you'll be entertained by 18C storytellers and balladeers. After dinner, go for "Gambols" (colonial card games) at Josiah Chowning's Tavern *(Duke of Gloucester St.)*.

and Mary★ *(west end of Duke of Gloucester St.; 757-221-4000; www.wm.edu)* had been recently founded. The new capital, named after England's King William III, centered on mile-long, unpaved Duke of Gloucester Street, anchored on the east by the colonial capitol and on the west by the college. The town rapidly grew into an important governmental center. From Virginia's House of Burgesses came some of the leading figures of the American Revolution—Peyton Randolph, George Washington, Thomas Jefferson and Patrick Henry. In 1780 the Virginia capital was moved to Richmond.

Capitol, Colonial Williamsburg

©The Colonial Williamsburg Foundation

Williamsburg languished until 1926, when John D. Rockefeller Jr. provided the funding for scholars and archaeologists to began reconstructing the colonial town. Today, Colonial Williamsburg includes 88 original shops, houses and public buildings and hundreds of reconstructed colonial structures on their original sites.

Capitol★★★ – *East end of Duke of Gloucester St.* Originally completed in 1705 (the current building is a reconstruction), the Capitol is shaped like an H, symbolizing the bicameral system of British colonial government. Elected burgesses sat on the sparely decorated east side of the building, and the royal governor and his council convened on the ornate west side.

Raleigh Tavern★★ – *Duke of Gloucester St., one block west of the capitol.* In its heyday, Raleigh Tavern stood at the pivot of the capital's social life, welcoming regulars George Washington, Thomas Jefferson and Peyton Randolph.

Governor's Palace★★★ – *North end of Palace Green.* With its elegant woodwork, period furnishings and an incomparable orna-

EXCURSIONS

119

Michie Tavern★
683 Thomas Jefferson Pkwy. 434-977-1234. www.michietavern.com.
On your way up the mountain to Monticello, make a stop at Michie Tavern (established in 1784) for a trip back in time. Inside the rambling white structure you can feast colonial-style on the "ordinary," a set midday meal of fried chicken, stewed tomatoes, black-eyed peas, biscuits and cornbread.

mental display of 18C firearms, this reconstruction of the 1722 royal governor's palace was the most impressive building of its era in the colonies. Kids will love the **boxwood maze** that lies behind the palace.

George Wythe House★★ –
West side of Palace Green.
This original 18C Georgian brick residence was home to George Wythe (1726–1806), Virginia's most respected jurist and the College of William and Mary's first law professor.

DeWitt Wallace Gallery★★ –
S. Henry & Francis Sts.757-229-1000.
Located on the lower level of the historic Public Hospital, the gallery is renowned for its collection of English and American pieces dating from 1600 to 1830.

Abby Aldrich Rockefeller Folk Art Center★★ –
On S. England St., next to the Williamsburg Inn. 757-220-7670. Named for the wife of John D. Rockefeller Jr., the center boasts one of the finest collections of American folk art in the world.

Monticello★★★

125mi southwest of DC. Take I-66 West to US-29 South to Charlottesville. Follow Rte. 250 West/29 Bypass South to I-64 East; turn left on Rte. 53 and follow signs. 434-984-9822. www.monticello.org. Open Mar–Oct daily 8am–5pm, Nov–Feb daily 9am–4:30pm. Closed Dec 25. $15.

Thomas Jefferson seemingly never did anything halfway. The mountaintop home that Jefferson designed for himself outside Charlottesville, Virginia now ranks as the only house in the US on the

Monticello

©Brenda Klinger/Bigstockphoto.com

UNESCO World Heritage List of international treasures. Best known as the author of the Declaration of Independence, Jefferson held positions including governor of Virginia, minister to France, secretary of State, vice president and third US president (1801–09). Jefferson, an accomplished draftsman, musician and naturalist, began building his home in 1768 on the little mountain ("Monticello") that still commands fine views of the countryside. Upon returning from a five-year assignment as minister to France in 1796, Jefferson enlarged the house from 8 to 21 rooms and crowned the west entrance with a dome.

Visit – At the visitor center at the base of the mountain *(Rte. 20, just south of I-64, Exit 121; 434-977-1783)* you can view an introductory film, and a number of interesting Jefferson artifacts. Tours begin in the entrance hall, which Jefferson used as a museum. Inside, you'll see thoughtful innovations at every turn, from heat-conserving double doors to skylights and a dumbwaiter. After the tour, be sure to explore the all-weather passageway underneath the house, leading to the wine cellar and kitchen.

Charlottesville★★

125mi southwest of DC via I-66 West to US-29 South. Tourist information: 434-293-6789, 877-386-1103 or www.charlottesville tourism.org.

Set amid the eastern foothills of the majestic Blue Ridge Mountains and surrounded by the lush horse farms of Albemarle County, this university town was founded as the county seat in 1762. Well removed from Virginia's more established aristocracy, the area fostered a tough self-reliance that would produce several state and national leaders, including three of the country's first five presidents— Thomas Jefferson (1801–09), James Madison (1809–17) and James Monroe (1817–25). In addition to Jefferson's Monticello, **Ash Lawn-Highland★** *(Rte. 53, east of Rte. 20; 434-293-9539; www.*

Where To Stay

Boar's Head Inn *200 Ednam Dr., off Rte. 250 West, Charlottesville, VA. 434-296-2181 or 800-476-1988. www.boarsheadinn.com. 171 rooms. $175–$300.* This 573-acre estate offers 20 tennis courts, 4 pools, a golf course, a fitness facility and a full-service spa. Seventeenth-century antiques create a pub-like feel in the common areas, while spacious guest rooms feature four-poster beds and damask duvets. Of the inn's four restaurants, the **Old Mill Room** offers award-winning fine dining.

Keswick Hall *701 Club Dr., Keswick, VA. 434-979-3440 or 800-274-5391. www.keswick.com. 48 rooms. Over $200.* You'll think you're on an English country estate when you arrive at stately Keswick Hall. Located just minutes from Monticello, the Italianate mansion sports Laura Ashley fabrics and wall coverings. An 18-hole Arnold Palmer golf course lies at your doorstep, along with swimming, tennis and spa treatments. **Fossett's Restaurant** serves memorable regional American cuisine that changes with the season.

ashlawnhighland.org) preserves the remains of Monroe's tobacco plantation, and **Montpelier**★★ *(24mi northeast of Charlottesville via Rte. 20; 540-672-2728; www. montpelier.org)* gives visitors a look at Madison's former estate. Be sure to visit one of the many excellent **wineries** (and their tasting rooms!) in the surrounding countryside. *Check out www. monticellowinetrail.com for ideas of places to visit and their opening times and charges.*

University of Virginia★★

US-29 & US-250 Business (Emmet St. & University Ave.), Charlottesville. 434-924-7969. www.virginia.edu.

Thomas Jefferson's retirement project, the University of Virginia is a carefully planned "academical village" and one of only four works of architecture in the country to be included on the UNESCO World Heritage List. Today the university, which began in 1817, enrolls some 18,000 students and ranks as one of the top universities in the eastern US. The heart of Jefferson's village, the graceful **Rotunda**★★★

(University Ave. & Rugby Rd.), completed in 1826, was patterned on the Pantheon in Rome. Stand on the south Rotunda steps where you'll have a sweeping view of the **Lawn**, flanked by colonnades that link student rooms with ten pavilions. Each pavilion is modeled after a different Greek or Roman temple and serves as a residence for university deans and distinguished professors.

Annapolis★★

31mi east of DC via US-50 East. 410-280-0445. www.visit-annapolis.org.

You can easily spend a day in Annapolis, Maryland drooling over the yachts tied up at the City Dock, poking around in the boutiques that crowd the surrounding blocks, and ogling the Naval Academy cadets in their crisp uniforms. But don't stop there—take some time to discover the rich history of this small city.

Established on the banks of the Severn River by Virginia Puritans in 1648, Annapolis became the seat of colonial government in 1694, and subsequently grew to be a

Rotunda, University of Virginia

©Bill Manning/iStockphoto.com

State House, Annapolis

"the Yard," as the academy grounds are called, includes **Bancroft Hall,** the 1906 Baroque structure in the center of campus that covers 27 acres and boasts 5mi of corridors. The tour also stops at the copper-domed **Navy Chapel★★**, modeled after the Hôtel des Invalides in Paris.

Before you leave, check out the U.S. Naval Academy Museum in Preble Hall, where you'll find a rare collection of 17C to 19C ship models★★ made in England, as well as other artifacts detailing the history of the Navy.

busy port. The city's 1779 redbrick **State House★** *(center of State Circle; 410-974-3400)* served as the US capitol between 1783 and 1784. It was here, on January 14, 1784, that the Continental Congress ratified the Treaty of Paris, officially ending the Revolutionary War.

- **Hammond Harwood House★★** *(19 Maryland Ave.; 410-263-4683; www.hammond harwoodhouse.org),* built by William Buckland in 1775, and **Chase-Lloyd House★** *(22 Maryland Ave.; 410-263-2723),* known for its split, cantilevered staircase, typify the elegant Georgian-style residences built in Annapolis in the 18C.

United States Naval Academy★ – *Armel-Leftwich Visitor Center, 52 King George St. 800-778-4260. www.navyonline.com.* Future officers in the US Navy and Marine Corps study on this peaceful, 338-acre campus established in 1845 along the Severn River and Spa Creek. The guided walking tour *(depart from the visitor center, inside Gate 1 on King George St.)* around

Navy Chapel

Baltimore's Inner Harbor★★

38mi northeast of DC. Take I-95 North to Exit 27 and continue north to Baltimore. Take Exit 53 onto I-395 and follow it until it ends; turn right on Conway St. to the Inner Harbor. 410-837-4636. www.southbaltimore.com/ innerharbor.

No matter what your age, you're bound to enjoy this glittering waterfront complex of shops,

EXCURSIONS

123

restaurants, museums and hotels (bounded by Pratt & Light Sts.). Rescued from its downtrodden state in the 1960s, Baltimore's harbor is now anchored on the northeast and southwest corners by the National Aquarium and the **Maryland Science Center** (601 Light St.; 410-685-5225; www.mdsci. org) respectively. In between, the twin glass pavilions of Harborplace overlook the brick pier where the 1854 "sloop-of-war" **USS Constellation** is docked and open for tours (410-539-1797; www. constellation.org). Inside Harborplace's pavilions, you'll find a festival of shops and eateries.
Camden Yards – The city's beloved Orioles play baseball on this lovely field, a few blocks west of the waterfront (333 W. Camden St.; 410-685-9800 or 888-848-2473, http://baltimore.orioles.mlb.com).

National Aquarium in Baltimore★★

Pier Three, 501 E. Pratt St. 410-576-3800. www.aqua.org. Open Mar–Jun & Sept–Oct daily 9am–5pm (Fri until 8pm). Jul–Aug Sun–Thu 9am–6pm, Fri & Sat 9am–8pm.

Nov–Feb daily 10am–5pm (Fri until 8pm). Closed Thanksgiving & Dec 25. $21.95; $12.95 for children 3–11.

More than 10,000 marine creatures occupy the habitats within Baltimore's star attraction. In the five-story Main Aquarium, you can see the country's largest collection of rays in **Wings in the Water★**, and walk down through four stories of sharks, corals and other reef denizens in the **Atlantic Coral Reef★**. Save time for the dolphin show that takes place in the adjoining Marine Mammal Pavilion (showtimes are assigned when you buy an admission ticket).

Baltimore Maritime Museum★

Ticket booth on Pier Three, next to the aquarium. 410-396-3453. www. baltomaritimemuseum.org. March-Oct 10am-5:30pm; Nov-Feb 10am-4:30pm. Some extended hours in the summer. Closed Thanksgiving, Dec 25 and Jan 1. $10.

This partially floating museum consists of four sites—three historic vessels and the **Seven Foot Knoll Lighthouse**—that are linked by the Inner Harbor.

Baltimore Inner Harbor

©Aimin Tang/iStockphoto.com

National Aquarium in Baltimore

©JamesWest/JWestProductions.com/National Aquarium in Baltimore

Harpers Ferry National Historic Park★★

55mi northwest of DC in Harpers Ferry, West Virginia. From DC, take I-270 North to Frederick, Maryland, then go south on US-340. 304-535-6029. www.nps.gov/hafe. Open year-round daily 8am–5pm. Closed Jan 1, Thanksgiving Day & Dec 25. $6.

You may not know that this tiny West Virginia town takes its name from builder Robert Harper, who settled at the junction of the Shenandoah and Potomac rivers in 1751. You've more likely heard Harpers Ferry associated with abolitionist **John Brown** (1800–1859).

In 1859 Brown led a 21-man "army of the liberation" into town, planning to seize weapons from the US Armory and Arsenal in Harpers Ferry to use in waging a guerrilla war against slavery from the nearby mountains. When federal troops arrived to stop the raid, Brown and some of his followers barricaded themselves in the brick fire-engine/guard house. On October 18, a storming party of Marines broke into Brown's "fort" and captured the raiders. Brown was tried and convicted of "conspiring with slaves to commit treason and murder." He was hanged in December 1859. Although Brown's raid failed, the incident inflamed

Wild, Wonderful West Virginia

With its location at the confluence of the Shenandoah and Potomac rivers, Harpers Ferry provides a great base for many a watery adventure. Canoeing, kayaking, white-water rafting and tubing trips all begin here. For information, contact one of these local outfitters:

River & Trail Outfitters – *888-446-7529; www.rivertrail.com.*
Historical River Tours – *410-489-2837; www.historicalrivertours.com.*
River Riders – *800-326-7238; www.riverriders.com.*
For landlubbers, the 2,000mi-long **Appalachian Trail** also runs through Harpers Ferry. In fact, the Appalachian Trail Conference Information Center is located right in town *(799 Washington St.; 304-535-6331; www.appalachiantrail.org).*

EXCURSIONS

tensions between the North and South and set the stage for a series of events that erupted two years later in the Civil War.

Information Center –
Shenandoah St. Here you can see exhibits outlining the town's history and pick up a copy of the *Lower Town Trail Guide* to 24 key historic sites clustered on narrow, hilly Shenandoah, High and Potomac streets. From Jefferson Rock, you'll enjoy the same view that Thomas Jefferson described in 1783 as being "worth a voyage across the Atlantic." When you're ready for a break from sightseeing, tackle the many shops that line High Street.

Skyline Drive★★

70mi west of DC via I-66. 540-999-3500. www.nps.gov/shen. Open year-round daily. $10/vehicle Dec–Feb; $15/vehicle March–Nov.

If you like scenic mountain drives, you'll love this one. Skyline Drive, the best-known feature within the more than 196,030 acres of **Shenandoah National Park★★**, traces the backbone of the Blue Ridge for 105mi as it runs through western Virginia. Girdled by low stone walls, 75 parking overlooks along the drive offer one dazzling view after another. To the east, the Piedmont's rounded hills slope down to the coastal plain.

The western peaks give way to the Shenandoah Valley, named for the river that winds lazily past fields, woods and farms. At Rockfish Gap, Skyline Drive hooks up seamlessly with the **Blue Ridge Parkway★★** and continues through North Carolina. The parkway ends in Cherokee near the entrance to **Great Smoky Mountains National Park★★★** *(865-436-1200; www.nsp.gov/grsm, $16).* In the fall the mountains come alive with the vibrant autumnal colors. It's one of the most spectacular ways to take in fall foliage and one of the most popular— the drive gets quite busy on weekends.

Skyline Drive begins at US-340, in Front Royal, Virginia. See map p126.

Skyline Caverns – *1mi south of park entrance on US-340, Front Royal, VA. 540-635-4545. www.sky linecaverns.com.* This 60-million-year-old limestone cave includes **Fairyland Lake★**, whose glassy surface shimmers in the glow of multicolored lights.

Front Royal to Thornton Gap – *31.5mi.* Skyline Drive climbs to **Shenandoah Valley Overlook**

Visiting Shenandoah National Park

The park is open year-round, though portions of Skyline Drive may be temporarily closed in winter due to weather conditions. Many of the park facilities are closed from late November through March. The speed limit in the park is 35mph. Concrete mile markers located on the west side of the road are numbered in increasing order from north to south. More than 500mi of trails lace the park, including 101mi of the **Appalachian Trail**, which runs from Maine to Georgia. Maps and free backcountry permits are available at the park headquarters in Luray, VA *(540-999-3500)* and at the park visitor centers: Dickey Ridge *(mile 4.6),* Harry F. Byrd *(mile 51),* and Loft Mountain *(mile 79.5).*

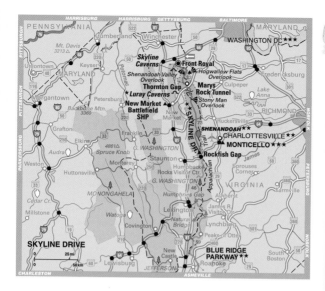

(mile 2.8), where the sweeping **view**★★ west takes in Massanutten Mountain. **Hogwallow Flats Overlook** (mile 13.8) looks east over lumpy peaks called monadnocks, remnants of a range that predates the Blue Ridge.

Luray Caverns★ – *9mi west of Thornton Gap Entrance on US-211, Luray, VA. 540-743-6551. www.luray caverns.com, $19.* Lying some 160 feet underground, popular Luray Caverns abounds with stalactites and flowstone that drips from above.

New Market Battlefield State Historical Park – *21mi west of Thornton Gap entrance on US-211, New Market, VA. 540-464-7334 www4.vmi.edu/museum.* (Closed Dec 23- Jan 3)On these bucolic pastures west of the Blue Ridge, 257 cadets from the Virginia Military Institute in Lexington helped defeat Union forces in May 1864.

Marys Rock Tunnel to Rockfish Entrance Station★★ – *73mi.* To create the short length of Marys Rock Tunnel (mile 32.4), workers drilled through more than 600 feet of rock for three months before the tunnel opened to traffic in 1932. From **Stony Man Overlook** (mile 38.6) you can see Old Rag, crowned in one-billion-year-old granite.

Skyline Drive ends at Rockfish Gap (mile 105.4), where two major east-west highways, US-250 and I-64, cross the mountains.

Frontier Culture Museum★★ – *5mi west of I-81 Exit 222 off US-250 West in Staunton, VA. 540-332-7850. www.frontiermuseum.org. Open mid-Mar–Nov daily 9am–5pm. Rest of the year daily 10am–4pm. $10.* Nestled in the farmlands of the Shenandoah Valley, this 78-acre outdoor living-history complex preserves the region's European

127

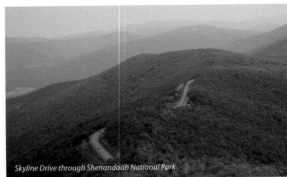
Skyline Drive through Shenandoah National Park

National Park Service

heritage through a series of 17–19C farm buildings that were dismantled and moved to this site.

Maryland's Eastern Shore★

50mi east of DC via US-50 East across the Chesapeake Bay Bridge. 866-639-3526, www.mdisfun.org.

Think sleepy fishing villages, small farms, and a low-lying coastline cut by quiet coves and lonely marshes. This is Maryland's Eastern Shore, a peninsula that lies between the Chesapeake Bay and the Atlantic Ocean, just across the Bay Bridge from Annapolis. You can easily while away a couple of pleasant days here exploring historic waterside villages such as **St. Michaels★** and Chestertown, staying in some of the fine bed-and-breakfast inns, bird-watching and poking through myriad antique shops. And while you're there, be sure to sample the region's bountiful seafood—especially the Chesapeake Bay's famous blue crabs *(in season Jun–Oct)*.
Pony Penning★ – One of the shore's most unique events takes place each summer on the southern end of **Assateague Island National Seashore★** *(29mi east of Salisbury, MD, via US-50 & Rte. 611; 410-641-1441; www.nps.gov/asis)*. This part of the 37mi-long barrier island harbors several hundred wild ponies that roam **Chincoteague National Wildlife Refuge** across the Maryland state line in Virginia. The offspring of horses brought here by 17C European settlers to avoid taxes, the ponies are rounded up annually on Assateague Island and

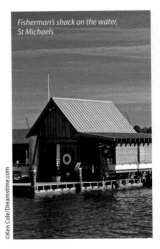
Fisherman's shack on the water, St Michaels

©Ken Cole/Dreamstime.com

MUST SEE

Inn at Perry Cabin

308 Watkins Lane, St. Michaels, MD. 78mi east of DC via US-50 East. 410-745-2200 or 866-278-9601. www.perrycabin.com. 81 rooms. Over $300.

This lovely white Colonial mansion was built on the banks of the Miles River just after the War of 1812 by Samuel Hambleton, aide-de-camp to Commodore Oliver Hazard Perry. Take a dip in the heated pool, borrow one of the inn's bikes and cycle around historic St. Michaels, or schedule a sailing trip or a fishing charter. At the end of the day, come back to relax in rooms decked out in English and early American antiques and Laura Ashley prints. The innovative American cuisine at **Sherwood's Landing** incorporates fresh local seafood.

herded across the narrow channel (at slack tide) to the town of Chincoteague *(across Chincoteague Bay on Rte. 175).* Here the annual Pony Penning, the public roundup and sale of foals, is held on the last Wednesday and Thursday of July *(for details, call 757-336-6161 or check online at www.chincoteague chamber.com).*

Berkeley Springs, West Virginia

About 100mi from Washington (about a 2 hour drive). I270 to Frederick, I70W to Rt 522. 800-447-8797 www.berkeleysprings.com.

The naturally occurring mineral springs here have earned Berkeley Springs the slogan "the nation's first spa." Early in America's history the town became a popular resort destination among those intrigued by tales of its healing waters and pretty scenery. (George Washington was among those who vacationed here.) Today the quaint

mountain town is a both a haven for artists, many of whom sell their wares in the shops on the main street, and a quiet retreat for city folk seeking a dose of small town living. At Berkeley Springs State Park visitors can experience the baths and warm spring waters that lured the founding fathers years ago. Separate men's and women's **Roman baths** are maintained by the park *($40 per 30 minutes; appointments necessary, 800-225-5982, www.berkeleyspringssp.com).* Water bubbles from the springs at a constant 74F and is heated by staff for the bathing. Massages may also be booked in conjunction with the baths.

At Nearby **Cacapon State Park** *(304-258-1022, www.cacaponresort. com)* visitors can reconnect with nature by taking advantage of its 6,000-square acres of hiking, boating, golf, swimming and winter sledding. Both cabins and rooms in the lodge can be reserved for overnight stays.

RESTAURANTS

The venues listed below were selected for their ambience, location and/or value for money. Rates indicate the average cost of an appetizer, an entrée and a dessert for one person (not including tax, gratuity or beverages). Most restaurants are open daily and accept major credit cards. Call for information regarding reservations, dress code and opening hours. Restaurants listed are located in Washington, DC, unless otherwise noted. For a listing of restaurants by theme (Power Lunches, Budget Beaters, etc.), see p142.

Luxury	**$$$$**	over $50	Moderate	**$$**	$15–$30
Expensive	**$$$**	$30–$50	Inexpensive	**$**	under $15

LUXURY

Ardeo

$$$$ **Northern Italian**
3311 Connecticut Ave, NW, Cleveland Park. 202-293-7191. www.ardeorestaurant.com.

Ardeo is one of those neighborhood restaurants with a big reputation and a who's who guest list. Happily the food lives up to the hype. The heirloom beets, avocado and baby tomatoes appetizer in a pomegranate reduction will get your palette stared. While the seared ahi tuna with mango, spring onions in a miso emulsion and the veal meatloaf with wild broccoli and Yukon Gold potato puree entrees will seal the deal. Rooftop terrace seating is a hard get but worth the wait on a pretty night. Next door, wine bar Bardeo serves wine flights and small plates

Bistro Bis

$$$$ **Modern French**
15 E Street, NW, Capitol Hill. 202-661-2700. www.bistrobis.com.

When Congress is in session, Bistro Bis becomes the unofficial lunchroom for many a member—not to mention the town's other power players trying to sway them. Chef and Owner Jeffrey Buben uses his culinary talents to interpret classic French bistro fare. The onion soup is a crowd pleaser as is the crisp braised pork belly with butter beans. The cheese course here rivals anything found in France. The restaurant's fromager selects more than 20 cheeses for the board each day, often incorporating small-production cheeses from all over the world and the United States into the mix.

The Caucus Room

$$$$ **American**
401 9th St. NW, Downtown. Closed Sun. 202-393-1300. www.thecaucusroom.com.

This is the consummate Washington steakhouse, where power players sink into the dark wooded interior and enjoy a tender steak and a glass of merlot. Truly a bipartisan venture, The Caucus Room is partially owned by notable Republican Haley Barbour and Democrat Tom Boggs, and boasts a colorful William Woodward mural of a jovial donkey and elephant amicably sharing a lavish feast. Generous portions and impeccable service justify the high prices.

Central Michel Richard

$$$$ Contemporary
*1001 Pennsylvania Avenue, NW.
202-626-0015 www.centralmichel
richard.com.*

Central Michel Richard

Chef Michel Richard latest culinary venture in the Washington area blends traditional cuisine with a re-laxed contemporary atmosphere. Many dishes tend to have a French influence. The chef's signature Ahi tuna burger doesn't disappoint, especially when served with crispy fries. A see through meat locker in the corner and glass enclosed color-coded wine cellars add hints of interest to the soothing com-fortable décor. Sip a Clementine mimosa or a mojito at the bar after a long day of touring.

Citronelle

$$$$ California French
*3000 M. St. NW, Georgetown.
Breakfast and dinner only. Closed
Sun in Jul & Aug. 202-625-2150.
www.citronelledc.com.*

Located in Georgetown's Latham Hotel, Citronelle brings the in-spired innovative cuisine of Michel Richard to DC from the West Coast. Nightly prix-fixe menus range from three courses to the elaborate eight-course Promenade Gourmande menu for $190. On any given night your appetizer choices might include the likes of escargots or artichoke terrine, and entrées ranging from black bass Barigoule to cote de boeuf with shallot sauce. Homemade petits fours appear at the end of every dinner. Jacket required.

CityZen

$$$$ New American
*1330 Maryland Ave. SW,
Downtown/Waterfront (in the
Mandarin Oriental Hotel). Dinner
only. Closed Sun & Mon. 202-787-
6006. www.mandarin-oriental.com.*

Bold award-winning Chef Eric Ziebold, disciple of superstar Thomas Keller, above all wants his patrons to have fun. His unquenchable zest for originality might start with an amuse-bouche of minced pumpkin topped with a scallop and dusted, tableside, with Sri Lankan cinnamon. On to the signature hot foie gras risotto accented with tart roasted apple, then a crisp-skinned black bass with a gratin of sunchokes and a lump of osetra caviar. Or

CityZen

Destination DC

reacquaint yourself with the cauliflower—lightly caramelized and swished in sweet garlic. CityZen also serves a variety of martinis and has a large collection of single malt whiskeys. Having fun yet?

Corduroy

$$$$ **New American**
1122 Ninth Street NW, Downtown. 202-289-8810. www.corduroydc.com.

If you don't know where to look, Corduroy can be hard to find. But once you do discover this gem of a restaurant you'll make a point of remembering how to get back. Located on the second floor of the Sheraton Four Points Hotel with no direct entrance of its own, the restaurant is owned by Chef Tom Power who studied under Michel Richard. Powers selects fresh, mostly local, ingredients and builds his dishes around them. Jackets are preferred for men and shorts and hats are not permitted.

Nora

$$$$ **New American**
2132 Florida Ave. NW, Dupont Circle. Dinner only. Closed Sun. 202-462-5143. www.noras.com.

Nora

America's first certified organic restaurant, Nora is housed in a 19C grocery store off Dupont Circle. Nora Pouillon's politically correct, New American menu (think roasted heirloom-tomato soup and pan-roasted wild Alaskan halibut with Sweet & Sour Eggplant Caponata and Lemon Thyme Broth) sits well with Washington diners, who have praised her innovative organic creations for 22 years.

Palena

$$$$ **New American**
3529 Connecticut Ave., NW, Cleveland Park. Closed Sun. 202-537-9250 www.palenarestaurant.com.

Former White House chefs Frank Ruta and Ann Amernick have combined their talents to produce this innovative restaurant. Seasonal menus of three, four, or five courses might begin with a seafood boudin with a fine velouté of parsley and Calasparra rice, and continue on to an entrée such as pan-roasted veal cheeks in a Provencal daube with olives, capers, cardoons and little onions. Finish with the likes of a cashew dacquoise, or (something that needs no translation) a simple plate of homemade cookies.

EXPENSIVE

Café Atlantico

$$$ **Latin American**
405 8th St. NW, Penn Quarter. 202-393-0812. www.cafeatlantico.com.

Lively and unconventional, Café Atlantico was considered conservative Washington's most daring

Café Atlantico/Think Food Group

Tuna Ceviche, Café Atlantico

restaurant when it first opened. The kitchen tastefully modifies Nuevo Latino flavors to suit Washington's conservative and liberal taste buds. Updated favorites, such as tuna and coconut ceviche, and conch fritters with a liquid heart are suitably paired with refreshing rum-based mojitos or cachaça-infused caipirinhas that really pack a punch. The "Latino dim sum" are definitely worth trying.

Cashion's Eat Place

$$$ **New American**
1819 Columbia Rd. NW, Adams Morgan. Closed Mon. 202-797-1819. www.cashionseatplace.com.

The down-home folksiness of Cashion's belies its sophisticated cuisine, and that's the way Mississippian Ann Cashion wants her restaurant to stay. Fresh produce accompanies such Southern-inspired offerings as New Orleans-style gumbo, grilled pork chops with maple-pecan butter, and spicy fried rabbit with Creole mustard sauce. A non-provincial attitude shows in dishes like Asian crispy fish in a chile-lime sauce, and pea-shoot-and-radish salad.

The bar's after dark menu served from midnight to 2am Fridays and Saturdays appeals to club hoppers.

Ceiba

$$$ **Latin American**
701 14th St. NW, Downtown. Closed Sun. 202-393-3983. www.ceibarestaurant.com

The owners of DC Coast and Ten-Penh have modernized traditional Latino fare and come out winners at this new restaurant. Furnishings and tiles from Central and South America and the Caribbean set the mood. Start with a sampler of four ceviches—grouper, shrimp, tuna, and striped bass—and follow with a chile relleno stuffed with rock shrimp and goat cheese. The feijoada, a Brazilian staple of pork, black beans, and greens, comes with orange slices and fried manioc flour. A "shooter" of thick hot chocolate expands on classic churros, fried dough topped with cinnamon. All meals end with a box of caramel popcorn, whether you ask for it or not.

DC Coast

$$$ **New American**
1401 K St. NW, Downtown. 202-216-5988. Closed Sun. www.dccoast.com.

A towering bronze mermaid sculpture greets hungry locals at this downtown hotspot. Housed in an Art Deco-era bank, the contemporary dining room features lantern-style chandeliers, oversized oval mirrors and spiral-shaped booths. Chef Jeff Tunks' tri-coastal specialties (Mid-Atlantic, Gulf and West) include tuna tartare chunks with lime and coconut milk, and

RESTAURANTS

pan-roasted wild rockfish with crispy polenta cake in lobster corn broth.

District ChopHouse

$$$ **American**
509 7th St. NW, Downtown. 202-347-3434. www.chophouse.com.

Carved out of an old bank building, the District ChopHouse serves what you would expect—thick steaks and smooth beers. Classics like filet mignon, New York strip, and Iowa pork chops come with a house salad and choice of starch. On the mezzanine level, a full-service scotch and bourbon bar caters to power brokers, who often get a game going at the hand-carved billiard tables before having a smoke in the cigar lounge.

Georgia Brown's

$$$ **Southern**
950 15th St. NW, Downtown. 202-393-4499. www.gbrowns.com.

Locals love this well-appointed downtown eatery for its Lowcountry dishes, which take Southern regional ingredients to new heights. For starters, try the she-crab soup or cornmeal-crusted catfish fingers, then chow down on the likes of Charleston Perlau (red rice mixed with andouille sausage and duck, topped with "heads-on" shrimp) or Southern fried chicken. Selections such as sautéed black-eyed pea cakes appeal to vegetarians. Georgia Brown's **Sunday brunch** is one of the most popular in town and serves up more food than most people eat in a week.

Jaleo

$$$ **Spanish**
480 7th St. NW, Downtown. 202-628-7949. www.jaleo.com.

Trendsetting and always crowded, Jaleo specializes in classic hot and cold Spanish tapas, or small plates, including the restaurant's acclaimed fried calamari with aioli, grilled chorizo and savory steamed mussels. A sure bet is one of chef José Andrés' signature paellas, made with Calasparra rice, considered the best in Spain. Unique paella combinations here include lobster and chicken, squid and monkfish, and even a vegetarian version. On Wednesday nights, Flamenco dancers weave their sultry way around the tables. Jaleo now has additional locations in Bethesda and Crystal City.

Kinkead's

$$$ **New American**
2000 Pennsylvania Ave. NW, Downtown. 202-296-7700. www.kinkead.com.

Chef Bob Kinkead's award-winning American brasserie focuses on fresh seafood. Cod with crab Imperial, Virginia ham and cheddar-cheese spoonbread; seared sea scallops with shellbean succotash, corn flan, sherry lobster butter and garlic spinach; and softshell crabs with garlic flan are just some of the delights you might find on the daily changing menu here. Braised lamb shanks and grilled rib eye will please serious meat-lovers. Save room for such goodies as chocolate dacquoise napped with cappuccino sauce or key-lime custard cake topped with tropical fruit salsa.

The Occidental Grill

$$$ American
1475 Pennsylvania Ave. NW,
Downtown. 202-783-1475.
www.occidentaldc.com.

One of Washington's most historic
restaurants, the Occidental cozies
up against the stately Willard Hotel,
near the White House. The classic
American menu features a simple,
tasty selection of grilled meats
and fish with cameo appearances
by a trendier Chilean sea bass and
marinated veal cheeks.

Rosa Mexicano

$$$ Middle Eastern
575 7th Street at F Street NW;
Penn Quarter. 202-783-5522.
www.rosamexicano.info.

Mention that you're on your way
to Rosa Mexicano and chances
are you'll be told to order the
pomegranate margarita and the
guacamole. The margaritas come
frozen and servers prepare the
guacamole tableside with a
traditional Mexican lava-rock mor-
tar and pestle. It's tempting to stop
there but then you'd miss out on
the rest of the impressive menu.
Right across from the Verizon
Center in downtown Penn Quarter,
the striking restaurant features
large wrap-around windows and
a beautiful blue-tiled wall that
sparkles as water cascades down
its front. A second area location of
the New York-based chain opened
at the National Harbor in late 2008.

Taberna del Alabardero

$$$ Spanish
1776 I St., NW, Downtown.
Closed Sun. 202-429-2200.
www.alabardero.com.

Since 1989 Taberna's high quality
inventive Spanish menu has gone
well beyond the expected paella
and tapas (both of which, by the
way, are well worth ordering).
Starters could include blue-veined
Cabrales cheese with Serrano ham
or chickpea stew; entrées range
from Spanish salt cod to sweet-
breads and wild mushrooms in a
sherry reduction. For dessert, the
fig parfait (ice cream with a hint of
bleu cheese) and French-toast-like
torrijas bring down the house.

TenPenh

$$$ Southeast Asian
1001 Pennsylvania Ave. NW,
Downtown. Closed Sun. 202-
393-4500. www.tenpenh.com.

The sumptuous décor and notable
flavors of one of Washington, DC's
most popular Asian restaurants
resulted from the chef's six-week
shopping and tasting journey
to Asia. Begin with the Thai-style
coconut and chicken soup with
portabella mushrooms before
moving on to the red Thai curry
prawns. Wash your meal down
with a glass of sake or ginger
limeade and save room for the
cinnamon sugar dusted donuts
with dark bittersweet chocolate
pudding for dessert.

RESTAURANTS

Vidalia

$$$ **Regional American**
1990 M St. NW, Downtown. 202-659-1990. www.vidaliadc.com.

With upscale versions of shrimp and grits and chicken and dumplings, Vidalia is an oasis of Southern comfort food in Washington's bustling business district. Vidalia's contemporary Southern design complements the warm cornbread and refreshing lemonade that accent a summer lunch. Try the signature roasted Vidalia onion in season, and end your meal with sticky pecan pie topped with bourbon-laced ice cream.

MODERATE

Bangkok Bistro

$$ **Thai**
3251 Prospect St. NW, Georgetown. 202-337-2424. www.bangkok bistrodc.com.

The smooth lines and soothing violet and green colors of Bangkok Bistro won an award from Architectural Digest. With its outdoor cafe and garden seating, the Georgetown restaurant invites a lively summer dining crowd, while the fiery Thai flavors sizzle all year long. Bangkok Bistro eschews potent chiles for subtler flavors in its best dishes.

Cafe Deluxe

$$ **American**
3228 Wisconsin Ave. NW, Cleveland Park. 202-686-2233. www.cafedeluxe.com.

With the feel of a trendy brasserie, Cafe Deluxe eases patrons into a menu of traditional comfort foods. Soothing, dark booths provide a relaxing backdrop for the grilled meatloaf with Creole sauce and applewood-smoked pork chops, while the contrasting Art Deco décor complements new renditions of old cocktails, such as Imperial martinis, made with a splash of chambord. Cafe Deluxe keeps vegetarians happy with generous salads, pastas and pizzas smothered with vegetables and cheese. Gooey apple pie with caramel sauce will please most any sweet tooth. Happily for parents, the kids menu here goes beyond macaroni and cheese and comes with a small bucket of crayons.

Clyde's of Georgetown

$$ **American**
3236 M St. NW, Georgetown. 202-333-9180. www.clydes.com.

With several locations in the Washington metropolitan area, cheery, saloon-like Clyde's has burgeoned into a Washington legend. Casual diners can opt for traditional burgers, sandwiches and chili, while patrons with greater expectations can select from a lengthy list of fashionable martinis and fresh sea-

Ron Blunt/Clyde's of Georgetown

Clyde's of Georgetown

food. The vintage transportation theme gives the eye many places to look while your food is cooking.

The Diner

$$ American
2453 18th Street NW, Adam's Morgan. 202-232-8800. www.trystdc.com/diner.

The name says it all. Order what you want when you want it. Breakfast at 4 in the afternoon, no problem. Pie with your morning coffee, no one will lift an eyebrow. A slightly funky version of an old school diner and one of the few places in town open 24-hours a day, seven days a week. Tryst Coffeehouse *(2459 18th Street NW)* a couple of doors down is owned by the same people and a great spot to people watch.

Heritage India

$$ Indian
2400 Wisconsin Ave., NW, Glover Park. 202-333-3120. www. heritageindiaofgeorgetown.com. Second location at 1337 Connecticut Ave., NW, near Dupont Circle 202-331-1414. www.heritageindia dupont.com.

One of Washington's top Indian restaurants continues to cook superb variations on Indian themes. Lamb simmered in yogurt and saffron; grouper with onions, tomatoes, and green peppers; and a number of tandoori dishes masterfully blend spices and textures. The Dupont Circle kitchen pushes into new territory with mezzes of smoked mozzarella, hummus of roasted garlic and black beans, and meat kebabs—anything that fits on a small plate.

Lauriol Plaza

$$ Mexican
1835 18th St. NW, Dupont Circle. 202-387-0035. www.lauriol plaza.com.

One of Dupont Circle's most popular and affordable eateries, Lauriol Plaza serves up some of the best margaritas in town. Fabulous fajitas and other Tex-Mex mainstays are joined by Puerto Rican and Latin American selections on the extensive menu. With ample outdoor dining, Lauriol Plaza sizzles on summer evenings.

Lebanese Taverna

$$ Middle Eastern
2641 Connecticut Ave. NW, Woodley Park. 202-265-8681. www.lebanesetaverna.com.

A Woodley Park favorite, Lebanese Taverna teems with young professionals and outdoor cafe enthusiasts. Go with a group and order a savory array of mezze, a spread of hors d'oeuvres, paired with the warm, soft pita bread that emerges from the wood-burning ovens. If you crave something more hearty, try the juicy rotisserie chicken or the lemony chicken shish taouk. Vegetarians will love this menu.

Meiwah Restaurant

$$ Chinese
1200 New Hampshire Ave. NW, Downtown. 202-833-2888. www.meiwahrestaurant.com.

It doesn't get much better than the steamed dumplings, tofu curl and garlic eggplant at this favorite DC haunt. Owner Larry La also founded one of the city's other popular Chinese restaurants, City Lights of China. Meiwah does a bustling dine-in and take-out—and happily delivers to nearby hotels.

Old Europe

$$ German
2434 Wisconsin Ave. NW, Georgetown. Closed Mon. 202-333-7600. www.old-europe.com.

One of Washington's few German restaurants, Old Europe draws a healthy contingency of beer and schnitzel lovers who find solace in few other locales. The walls are covered, as you might expect, with steins and wooden crests that create a perpetual air of Oktoberfest. Satisfying, stick-to-your-ribs dishes are served up in short order by the friendly waitstaff.

Old Glory

$$ Barbecue
3139 M St. NW, Georgetown. 202-337-3406. www.oldglorybbq.com.

Don't miss this lively barbecue joint perched on the busy Georgetown corner of M Street and Wisconsin Avenue. Settle into a booth, and a server will promptly arrive to "brand" your table with a purposeful slap of an iron stamp. Each table comes equipped with six regionally inspired sauces to suit patrons' preferences. Mosey up to the lavish hickory bar, where you'll find one of the largest s elections of bourbons in DC. Kids go for the draft root beer.

Tackle Box

$$ Seafood
3245 M St., NW, Georgetown. 202-337-8269. www.tacklebox-dc.com.

One of the new players on the DC food scene, the Tackle Box bills itself as Washington DC's first and only lobster shack. Catfish, bay scallops, shrimp, clams, oysters, calamari, bluefish, tilapia and rainbow trout all made it on the menu, often more than once. Many items are deep fried or wood grilled. Sides include house cut fries, sweet potato fries, mac & cheese, mashed potatoes, grilled asparagus and grilled corn. Choose from blueberry pie or brownies for dessert. The restaurant prides itself on supporting suppliers who use habitat-friendly fishing gear buys its produce from local farmers

Tony Cheng's Seafood Restaurant

$$ Chinese
619 H St., NW, Chinatown. 202-371-8669.

Long considered one of the city's best Chinese restaurants, this busy Hong Kong-style eatery is versatile enough to do Hunan, Szechuan, and dim sum—and do them all well. You can't go wrong with the Dungeness crab or whole fish straight from the tank at the entrance. Other possibilities include duck in spicy garlic sauce, and shrimp and asparagus in black bean sauce. The widest selection of dim sum is available on weekends, served from rolling carts.

Tortilla Coast

$$ Tex-Mex
*400 First St. SE, Capitol Hill.
Closed Sun. 202-546-6768.
www.tortillacoast.com.*

Wayward Texans have found their
way to Tortilla Coast for potent
margaritas and spicy tastes of
home since 1988. Cleanse your
palate with the Stars and Stripes
margarita, a blend of traditional
and strawberry margaritas laced
with Blue Curacao. Southwest-
ern flavors shine through in the
hickory barbecue chicken fajitas,
while spinach and mushroom
enchiladas satisfy vegetarians.

Zaytinya

$$ Mediterranean
*701 9th St. NW (at G St.),
Penn Quarter. 202-638-0800.
www.zaytinya.com.*

Both the food and the color
scheme at Zaytinya evoke the sun-
drenched Mediterranean region.
Opened in 2002 by Jaleo chef José
Andrés, the boisterous restaurant
still draws rave reviews. Savor small
servings (mezze) of braised rabbit
with lentils, and cured Turkish loin
of beef, or splurge on the fresh fish
of the day, grilled whole. Desserts
meld exotic flavors in the likes of

Octopus Santorini, Zaytinya

Zaytinya/Think Food Group

Medjool dates roasted in vin santo
(sweet wine) with orange short-
bread and olive-oil ice cream.

INEXPENSIVE

Amsterdam Falafelshop

$ Falafel
*2425 18th Street NW;
Adam's Morgan. 202-234-1969.
www.falafelshop.com*

Amsterdam Falafelshop

Amsterdam Falafelshop's popular-
ity makes it hard to get a table but
after one bite—even if half of it
winds up on your shirt because
you are propped up against a
wall—you won't mind.
Here's the drill: you can order a
falafel sandwich (half or whole),
fries, a brownie, soda and/or
lemonade. Once you get your
sandwich you top it yourself with
the salads, sauces, veggies and
other two dozen or so toppings at
the counter. But you only get one
shot at filling up your pita. There
are no return trips to the toppings
bar (really, try it and get the hairy
eyeball or worse) so people get
creative in how they approach
their sandwiches. Mayo, homemade peanut sauce, malt vinegar,
Old Bay Seasoning and ketchup

are on hand for the twice-cooked Dutch-style fries.

🍴 Ben's Chili Bowl

$ **Chili**
1213 U St. NW, U Street Area. 202-667-0909. www.benschilibowl.com.

Ben's is the common meeting ground for DC's traditional African-American community and young urban dwellers. Sloppy chili dogs, thick milkshakes and fries loaded with cheese and chili are universal pleasers in this Washington landmark, which retains the nostalgic charm of a 1950s diner.
Comedian Bill Cosby's favorite is the signature chili half-smoke.

Ben's Chili Bowl
Destination DC

Bread Line

$ **American**
1751 Pennsylvania Ave., NW, Downtown. Lunch only. Closed Sun and Sat). 202-822-8900.

Washington's savvy lunch crowd keeps the Bread Line moving well into the afternoon. What with knishes, empanadas, pizzas, grilled breads, and great sandwiches, this restaurant covers the field when it comes to bread. The summer BLTs are a popular choice, as are the barbecue sandwiches. There are always two soup options, six salads, and a variety of pastries.

Brickskeller

$ **American**
1523 22nd St. NW, Dupont Circle. 202-293-1885. www.thebrickskeller.com.

Even before microbreweries were the rage, this simple bar with checkered tablecloths was well known to beer aficionados. Its drink menu—more like a booklet—is broken down by countries, with all available beers from a particular nation listed.
The hundreds of brews served range from Belgium Trappist ale to Lebanese Almaza. Little wonder that owner Dave Alexander holds the Guiness world record for the "most varieties of beer commercially available."

Firehook Bakery & Coffeehouse

$ **Bakery**
3411 Connecticut Ave. NW, Cleveland Park. 202-362-2253. www.firehook.com. Check website for other locations.

For a quick, tasty sandwich or a sugary snack, Firehook Bakery captures carbohydrate fiends with its tempting window displays. Mini-loaves of fresh, crusty bread compliment fresh mozzarella and pesto on a simple tomato and mozzarella sandwich, while cream-filled tarts beg to be taken home from behind old-fashioned glass cases. Take your treat outside to the large patio and forget you are in the city for a few minutes.

MUST EAT

Nooshi

$ Asian
1120 19th St. NW, Downtown. 202-293-3138. www.nooshidc.com.

The former Oodles Noodles adds sushi to its menu, playfully fusing Malaysian, Japanese, Indonesian, Thai and Chinese variations of noodles. Select from udon, ramen, egg, and chow fun noodles, then select a preparation style—the frenzied cooks do the rest. Savory satays and chicken-coconut soup are worthy introductions to a quick, simple menu.

Pizzeria Paradiso

$ Pizza
2029 P St. NW, Dupont Circle. 202-223-1245. www.eatyourpizza.com.

Tucked inside a tiny row house, Pizzeria Paradiso marries delicate crusts and fresh ingredients to create one of the best pizzas in town. The exceptional crust soaks in a smoky flavor from the wood-burning oven, as fresh mozzarella melts over a bed of sliced roma tomatoes. And customers are happy to wait in line for a table to sample it. Paradiso's new Georgetown location is twice as big as the original place *(3282 M St. NW; 202-337-1245).*

Rockland's Barbeque and Grilling Company

$ Barbecue
2418 Wisconsin Ave. NW, Georgetown. 202-333-2558. www.rocklands.com.

For a quick, inexpensive meal in upper Georgetown, follow the sweet smell of hickory smoke up Wisconsin Avenue to Rockland's.

Traditional barbecue staples, from ribs and chopped pork to jalapeño cornbread, are deftly handled here. If you're shopping for something a little different, try the smoky grilled catfish or salmon sandwich.

Saigonnais

$ Vietnamese
2307 18th St. NW, Adams Morgan. 202-232-5300. www.dcnet.com/saigonnais.

Located in the heart of Adams Morgan, Saigonnais tantalizes with aromatic Indochine creations. Stylish and simple, the spring rolls are crisp and flavorful, while the pork-filled crêpe rolls (some assembly required) offer a challenging prelude to the suave lemongrass chicken and other generous dishes. The walls of the tiny restaurant are covered with photos of celebrity patrons.

Morty's Delicatessen

$ Deli
4620 Wisconsin Avenue, NW, Tenleytown. 202.686.1989. www.mortysdc.com.

Overstuffed pastrami on rye, matzo balls that could be used for pitching practice and a river of smoked fish is what keeps regulars coming back over and over again to one of DC's few New York style delis. You can order eggs and other breakfast items all day long and bowls of pickles get refilled throughout your meal. And, what the restaurant lacks in ambiance it makes up in portion size. A take out counter in front also sells cheesecake, rugalach and black and white cookies.

RESTAURANTS

RESTAURANTS BY THEME

Looking for a place for that power lunch, or a restaurant that serves Sunday brunch? In the preceding pages, we've organized the eateries by price category, so below we've broken them out by theme to help you plan your meals while you're in town.

Budget Beaters

Ben's Chili Bowl (p140)
Bread Line (p140)
Brickskellar (p140)
Firehook Bakery & Coffeehouse (p140)
Nooshi (p141)
Pizzeria Paradiso (p141)
Rockland's Barbeque & Grilling Company (p141)
Saigonnais (p141)

Ethnic Experiences

Bangkok Bistro (p136)
Café Atlantico (p132)
Heritage India (p137)
Jaleo (p134)
Lauriol Plaza (p137)
Lebanese Taverna (p137)
Meiwah (p137)
Saigonnais (p141)
Taberna del Alabardero (p135)
TenPenh (p135)
Tony Cheng's Seafood Restaurant (p138)
Zaytinya (p139)

Citronelle

Citronelle

Restaurant Week

Twice a year you don't have to have a big expense account or deep pockets to eat like a CEO. Every January and August more than 100 of DC's best eateries put on Restaurant Week, where regular folk can sit down to a 3-course prix fixe dinner or lunch and still have money left to pay the rent. Lunch costs $20 and change that is calculated to reflect the year. So in 2008, lunch cost $20.08. The price tag for dinner is $30 plus the change. You can find out the exact dates and make Restaurant Week reservations—or reservations for the rest of the year—at www.opentable.com.

Federal City History
Ben's Chili Bowl (p140)
District Chophouse (p134)
Occidental Grill (p135)

For a Special Occasion
Ceiba (p133)
Citronelle (p131)
CityZen (p131)
Nora (p132)
Palena (p132)

Hip Décor
DC Coast (p133)
Rosa Mexicano (p135)
TenPenh (p135)
Zaytinya (p139)

In Georgetown
Bangkok Bistro (p136)
Citronelle (p131)
Clyde's of Georgetown (p136)
Old Europe (p138)
Old Glory (p138)
Rockland's Barbeque (p141)
Tackle Box (p138)

Neighborhood Joints
Ben's Chili Bowl (p140)
Brickskeller (p140)
Morty's Delicatessen (p141)
Pizzeria Paradiso (p141)
Saigonnais (p141)
Tortilla Coast (p139)

Power Lunches
Bistro Bis (p130)
Caucus Room (p130)
District Chophouse (p134)
Kinkead's (p134)
Vidalia (p136)

Small Plates/Tapas
Jaleo (p134)
Taberna del Alabardero (p135)
Zaytinya (p139)

Southern Hospitality
Ben's Chili Bowl (p140)
Cafe Deluxe (p136)
Cashion's Eat Place (p133)
Georgia Brown's (p134)
Vidalia (p136)

Well Known Chefs
Citronelle / Michel Richard (p131)
Corduroy / Tom Power (p132)
Jaleo /José Andrés (p134)
Kinkead's / Bob Kinkead (p134)
Nora / Nora Pouillon (p132)

Sunday Brunch
Cashion's Eat Place (p133)
Clyde's of Georgetown (p136)
Georgia Brown's (p134)
Old Glory (p138)

HOTELS

The properties listed below were selected for their ambience, location and/or value for money. Prices reflect the average cost for a standard double room for two people (not including applicable taxes). You can often find discounted rates on weekends and off-season. Properties are located in Washington, DC, unless otherwise specified. Quoted rates don't include the city's hotel tax of 14.5%. For a listing of hotels by theme (Posh Place, Budget Beaters, etc.), see p154.

Luxury	$$$$$	over $350	Inexpensive	$$	$100–$175
Expensive	$$$$	$250–$350	Budget	$	Under $100
Moderate	$$$	$175–$250			

LUXURY

Four Seasons Hotel

$$$$$ 211 rooms
2800 Pennsylvania Ave. NW, Georgetown. 202-342-0444 or 800-332-3442. www.fourseasons.com.

Hiding behind an unassuming brick exterior, this upscale hotel earns its distinguished marks for the luxury and impeccable service you'd expect from Four Seasons. Original art adorns the walls of the roomy suites, complementing the tony flavor of surrounding Georgetown. Take advantage of the state-of-the-art fitness center, or treat yourself to a massage at the spa.

Mandarin Oriental Hotel

$$$$$ 400 rooms
1330 Maryland Ave. SW, Southwest/Capitol Hill. 202-554-8588. www.mandarin-oriental.com.

Offering exquisite views of the marina and skyline, the Mandarin Oriental pioneers in both unconventional location and high price. Bowing to the business traveler, this high-end property spares no expense to offer the most luxurious hotel experience. Private balconies, Japanese artwork, walnut furnishings, Thai silk wall hangings, Chinese marble bathrooms, and flat-screen TVs make guests feel oh-so-appreciated. The hotel boasts one of the city's best spas.

Premier Room, Four Seasons Hotel

Destination DC

The Ritz-Carlton, Washington, DC

$$$$$ 300 rooms
1150 22nd St. NW, Foggy Bottom/West End. 202-835-0500 or 800-241-3333. www.ritzcarlton.com.

The Ritz brings sought-after amenities to the West End. Large rooms are bathed in mossy tones, with sumptuous bedding and upscale perks—an overnight shoe-shine and complimentary morning newspaper—which appeal to business travelers. The hotel underwent a $12 million renovation in 2008. Guests can work out and have a relaxing massage at the Sports Club/LA Splash sports complex *(see Must Be Pampered)*.

The St. Regis, Washington, DC

$$$$$ 175 rooms
16th & K Sts. NW, Downtown. 202-638-2626 or 877-787-3447. www.stregis.com/washington.

This elegant 1926 landmark hotel reopened in 2008 following an extensive renovation and restoration. Here every detail has been considered from the Pratesi linens on the beds to the BlackBerrys held by the personal butlers so you can email requests through

---

The Watergate Hotel

Famed for its part in the Nixon scandal, The Watergate *(2650 Virginia Ave. NW, West End; 202-965-2482 or 800-289-1555; www.thewatergatehotel.com)* is closed until late 2009 for an impressive $170 million renovation. The new-look hotel is expected to be one of Washington's most luxurious. Check the website for updates.

---

the day. Situated in Washington's thriving business district just steps from the White House, inside, it's a glorious window into Washington's history of politics and intrigue. Since the grand opening, every president has stopped by this hotel, which frequently hosts royal guests and rock stars (think Queen Elizabeth II and Mick Jagger).

EXPENSIVE

The Fairfax at Embassy Row

$$$$ 259 rooms
2100 Massachusetts Avenue NW, Embassy Row. 202-293-2100 or 888-625-5144. www.fivestaralliance.com.

A multimillion dollar facelift in 2008 has left this stately hotel with a new interior look and a new name. Formerly a Westin, The Fairfax at Embassy Row sits at the edge of Embassy Row near Dupont Circle and the entrance to Georgetown, which puts it steps away from shops, restaurants and nightlife. The historic 1927 building once served as Al Gore's childhood home. The hotel is now part of the Starwood Luxury Collection Hotels

The Fairmont Washington, DC

$$$$ 415 rooms
2401 M St. NW, Foggy Bottom. 202-429-2400 or 866-540 4505. www.fairmont.com.

The great outdoors reigns in the Fairmont, as sunlight pours through the glassed-in atriums where trees flourish. Ample guest rooms are clothed in elegant furnishings and sunny hues; posh executive suites are tailored to suit business travelers and to accommodate small meetings. Ideally located on the fringes of Georgetown, the Fairmont provides easy access to shops and restaurants.

Hotel George

$$$$ **139 rooms**
15 E St. NW, Capitol Hill. 202-347-4200. www.hotelgeorge.com.

David Phelps/Kimpton Group

Washington's hippest hotel stormed onto the DC scene in 1998 to the chagrin of hotel traditionalists and to the delight of style-hungry liberals. With vibrant colors and contemporary artistic tributes to the first President of the United States, the Hotel George's minimalist interior and its location near "The Hill" and Union Station have made it a staple of business and leisure travelers as well as celebrity guests. Politicos and Washington bigwigs savor gourmet French meals in a casual Art Moderne setting at the hotel's **Bistro Bis ($$$).**

Hay-Adams

$$$$ **145 rooms**
800 16th St, NW (16th & H Sts. NW), Downtown. 202-638-6600 or 800-853-6807. www.hayadams.com.

With a picturesque view of the Executive Mansion from its location across Lafayette Square, the Hay-Adams is closer to the White House than any other of Washington's grand-dame hotels. Steeped in Washington lore, this 1928 Renaissance-inspired beauty repeatedly houses world leaders and discerning travelers. Rooms reflect the tailored elegance of a private home; some have carved plaster ceilings and balconies overlooking Lafayette Square.

The Liaison Capitol Hill

$$$$ **343 rooms**
415 New Jersey Avenue, NW, Capitol Hill. 202-638-1616 or 866-246-2203. www.affinia.com.

The newest player on the Washington upscale hotel scene, The Liaison Capitol Hill helps disprove the notion that all DC hotels are cherrywood and antiques. The Affinia hotel works hard to create an urban vibe with its thoroughly modern decor and amenities. Guitars, hair diffusers, pillows, yoga mats, laptop chargers and in-room spa treatments are among the items that can be ordered up from the pillow top menu in each room. The hotel's restaurant, Art and Soul, serves "Southern soul food."

The Mansion on O Street

$$$$ **39 rooms**
2020 O St. NW, Dupont Circle. 202-496–2020. www.omansion.com.

The Mansion on O Street is one part boutique hotel, one part art museum, one part private club and about one thousand parts whimsy. Each room in the eclectic luxury hotel is decorated with treasures collected from around the world so you will find a Mahogany

Rooftop pool, The Liaison Capitol Hill

Affinia Hotels

bed from Milan in one room and a teak Japanese-style soaking tub in the bathroom of another. In the spirit of the Mansion's history as a rooming house for Hoover's G-men in the 30s, a strict privacy policy is adhered to by all staff.

Renaissance Mayflower Hotel

$$$$ 654 rooms
1127 Connecticut Ave. NW, Downtown. 202-347-3000 or 800-228-7697. www.marriott.com

Opened in 1925, the venerable Mayflower is a perennial favorite of frequent visitors.
The hotel flaunts the splendor of Washington's golden age along busy Connecticut Avenue, near museums, the White House, shops and restaurants. The lobby of Washington's largest luxury hotel is graced with Beaux-Arts furniture and gilded accents, while the guest rooms recall the gentility of a distant era with their marble bathrooms and antiques.
Afternoon tea at the Mayflower is an institution in itself so make sure you make a reservation. This hotel recently underwent an $11 million restoration project..

W Washington, DC

$$$$ 311 rooms
15th St. and Pennsylvania Ave., NW, Downtown. 202-661-2400. www.whotels.com. Scheduled to open in summer 2009.

What used to be the Hotel Washington is due to re-open as a plush W hotel in June 2009. With one of the best views in Washington atop its rooftop bar and terrace and only a block and half from the White House, the location cannot fail to please. Add to this a state-of-the-art fitness center, a spa, and world class signature restaurant, we are sure this place will be a hit.

Washington Court Hotel

$$$$ 267 rooms
525 New Jersey Ave. NW, Capitol Hill. 202-628-2100 or 800-321-3010. www.washingtoncourthotel.com.

Luxurious suites offer an unparalleled view of the Capitol dome in this charming Capitol Hill hotel. Independently operated, the Washington Court Hotel provides easy access to Washington's monuments, attractions and restaurants. There's even a full

HOTELS

business center in the lobby and a state-of-the-art fitness room on the third floor.

Willard InterContinental

$$$$ 332 rooms
1401 Pennsylvania Ave. NW, Downtown. 202-628-9100 or 800-827-1747. www.washington. interconti.com.

A bastion of Washington tradition, the Willard towers over historic Pennsylvania Avenue two blocks from the White House. Inside, the dreamy Beaux-Arts lobby fosters political mystique with its grand columns and glittering chandeliers. The Round Robin Bar has served many a president mint juleps and potent brandies. Rooms reflect a tasteful, antique-drenched opulence, complete with views of the Washington skyline.

MODERATE

Beacon Hotel and Corporate Quarters

$$$ 197 rooms
1615 Rhode Island Ave. NW, Downtown. 202-296-2100 or 800-821-4367. http://capitalhotelswdc.com.

A $20 million renovation transformed the old Governor's House Hotel into this high-dollar player in the business-traveler market. With a focus on roominess and comfort, the Beacon eschews the frills of boutiquedom in favor of a more traditional luxury. Rooms feature up-to-date technology—flat-screen TVs, WebTV, Wi-Fi access—and guests can relieve stress in the state-of-the-art fitness center, or enjoy the large health club across the street.

Georgetown Suites

$$$ 217 rooms
1111 30th St. NW, Georgetown. 202-298-7800 or 800-348-7203. www.georgetownsuites.com.

Perfect for families and long-term visitors, this all-suite hotel is just minutes from historic Georgetown's shops and restaurants. Spacious comfortable suites come with fully equipped kitchenettes generously outfitted with microwaves, dishwashers and icemakers. Contemporary furnishings and soft tones characterize the soothing décor.

Hotel Helix

$$$ 178 rooms
1430 Rhode Island Ave. NW, Logan Circle. 202-462-9001 or 800-706-1202. www.hotelhelix.com.

A pop-art-style boutique hotel, the Helix greets you with a playful Magritte-esque mural out front. Vibrant in-room colors include cherry-red ottomans and royal-blue settees, while sheer drapes enclose platform beds. Special Zone Rooms feature soft microfiber chairs, lava lamps, and plasma-screen TVs; Bunk Rooms give kids the space they—and you—need.

Henley Park Hotel

$$$ 96 rooms
926 Massachusetts Ave. NW, Downtown. 202-638-5200 or 800-222-8474. www.henleypark.com.

The Henley Park Hotel's Tudor-style exterior and meticulously restored rooms reflect the classic elegance of Washington's earlier days. Less than a block from the Washington

MUST STAY

Convention Center, the Henley Park offers complimentary limo service to downtown or Capitol Hill. Gargoyles guard the entrance to this charming hotel, which prides itself on attentive service and is included on the Historic Hotels of America registry.

Jurys Washington

$$$ **315 rooms**
1500 New Hampshire Ave. NW, Dupont Circle. 202-483-6000 or 866-534-6857. www.jurysdoyle.com.

Flanking Washington's beloved Dupont Circle, Jurys Washington boasts spacious guest rooms complete with technological amenities geared to business travelers, including a business center, voice mail and a trouser press. Along the circle, Dupont Grille and Biddy Mulligan's bar reflect the hotel's Irish ownership, complementing the cosmopolitan neighborhood spirit.

The Latham Hotel

$$$ **133 rooms**
3000 M St. NW, Georgetown. 202-726-5000 or 800-368-5922. www.thelatham.com.

With a primo Georgetown location that houses **Citronelle** *(see Must Eat)*, one of Washington's most revered restaurants, the Latham sports comfy guest rooms and rambling suites designed to impress. The hotel boasts nine unique, two-story carriage suites and elegantly appointed guest rooms complete with terrycloth robes, marble baths, large desks and shaving mirrors. The rooftop swimming pool is especially appealing during the humid summer months.

The Madison Hotel

$$$ **391 rooms**
15th & M Sts. NW, Downtown. 202-862-1600 or 800-424-8577. www.themadisonhotel.net.

Perhaps better known for its graceful collection of antiques, the Madison proudly markets itself as "Washington's Correct Address." Located just a few blocks from the White House, the hotel's guest rooms are beautifully decorated with custom-made Federal-style furnishings. The Madison, now a Loews Hotel, reopened in August 2003 following a $30 million renovation.

The Melrose Hotel

$$$ **240 rooms**
2430 Pennsylvania Ave. NW, Foggy Bottom. 202-955-6400 or 800-635-7673. www.melrosehotel.com.

Sporting a catchy new name and fresh look, the Melrose reopened its doors in Foggy Bottom after an extensive remodeling project. The rooms bespeak comfortable luxury, while nightly rates have not raced to catch up. Located near George Washington University within walking distance of the Kennedy Center and Georgetown, the Melrose's cheery rooms are a Washington bargain.

Hotel Monaco

$$$ **183 rooms**
700 F St. NW, Downtown/Penn Quarter. 202-628-7177 or 800-649-1202. www.monaco-dc.com.

Located in the trendy Penn Quarter downtown, the Monaco occupies the restored all-marble 1893 Neoclassical Tariff Building. In the guest rooms, you'll find 15-foot ceilings and sunny yellow walls accented by bright contemporary furnishings. The National Portrait Gallery is right across the street, as is the sports and entertainment megaplex, the Verizon Center. Pets are welcome here, but if Fido couldn't make the trip, you can have a goldfish delivered to your room to keep you company. Oh-so-chic **Poste ($$$),** an American brasserie next door, provides 24-hour room service.

Hotel Monticello of Georgetown

$$$ 47 suites
1075 Thomas Jefferson St. NW, Georgetown. 202-337-0900 or 800-388-2410. www.monticello hotel.com.

The newly-renovated Hotel Monticello's ample, sunny suites brim with European charm and Georgetown sophistication. Just footsteps from the starting point of the historic C&O Canal and lively Wisconsin Avenue, the Monticello provides an excellent base for exploring Georgetown. You'll find Fluffy robes and slippers waiting for you in the marble bathrooms, and room rates include a continental breakfast with Starbucks coffee.

Morrison-Clark Inn

$$$ 54 rooms
1015 L St. NW, Downtown. 202-898-1200 or 800-332-7898. www.morrisonclark.com.

This turn-of-the-century mansion seems misplaced in the middle of downtown's business district. Past the antiques-filled parlor, with lace curtains and burgundy wall coverings, you'll find three styles of accommodations. Choose from neutral-toned Neoclassical, opulent Victorian, and country-style with distressed woods and wicker. Seasonal American cuisine at the inn's lovely **restaurant ($$$)** has made it a local favorite.

Omni Shoreham Hotel

$$$ 834 rooms
2500 Calvert St, NW, Woodley Park/Upper Northwest. 202-234-0700 or 800-545-8700. www. omnihotels.com.

Walk into the Omni's sprawling art deco-and-Renaissance style lobby and you'll start to see why the historic hotel has played host to every inaugural ball since its 1930 opening. Nestled on 11 acres of Rock Creek Park, the Omni offers the opportunity to have a bit of green and quiet while still being in the city and near a Metro line. A recent $15 million renovation included all of the guestrooms. If you check in here with your kids they likely will love the outdoor pools, bike rentals, weekly movie nights, the sweet guide dog who trains at the hotel (ask the concierge if the pup will do story time with your little ones) and the fact that the hotel is in walking distance to the National Zoo.

One Washington Circle

$$$ 151 rooms
One Washington Circle. NW, Foggy Bottom. 202-872-1680 or 800-424-9671. www.thecirclehotel.com.

Politicians, CEOs and artists have all overnighted at One Washington Circle. An all-suite hotel, this business-friendly property recently emerged from a multimillion-dollar makeover and looks spiffier than ever. Located between the White House and Georgetown, the hotel is a mere half-block from the Foggy Bottom Metro, and an easy walk to the Kennedy Center and State Department. An outdoor pool and private balconies give this one an edge over larger competitors.

INEXPENSIVE

Adam's Inn

$$ 26 rooms
1744 Lanier Pl. NW, Adams Morgan. 202-745-3600 or 800-578-6807. www.adamsinn.com.

A charming pension on a leafy residential street conveniently located seven blocks from the Woodley Park Metro, the Adam's is the kind of place you'd expect to find in Paris or Madrid. The inn encompasses three Victorian buildings. A wide porch leads to cheerful public rooms; tastefully furnished bedrooms let in lots of sunlight. Rates include a hearty continental breakfast.

Akwaaba

$$ 8 rooms
1708 16th St. NW, Dupont Circle. www.akwaaba.com. 877-893-3233.

Book lovers will feel right at home at Akwaaba, a cozy bed-and-breakfast style inn housed in an 1890s Dupont Circle townhouse. The inn celebrates African-American literature and each room is decorated in the theme of either a famous author like Toni Morrison

or Zora Neale Hurston or a literary genre. Author readings take place in the parlor from time to time and, not surprisingly, there is no shortage of reading material here.

Channel Inn Hotel

$$ 100 rooms
650 Water St. SW, Downtown/Waterfront. 202-554-2400 or 800-368-5668. www.channelinn.com.

Billed as Washington, DC's only waterfront hotel, the Channel Inn offers comfortable, affordable rooms with breathtaking views of the Washington Marina. Airy rooms offer full amenities and inviting balconies on which to watch graceful sailboats and river cruise ships glide past. DC's nearby fish market supplies the riverside hotel's **Pier 7 ($$$)** restaurant with the fresh catch of the day.

Doolittle Guest House

$$ 3 rooms
506 E. Capitol St. NE, Capitol Hill. 202-546-6622. www.doolittlehouse.com.

Though situated on a quiet, tree-lined street, this 1866 Victorian stands only four blocks from the US Capitol.
From here, guests can walk to almost all DC attractions, including the Smithsonian museums on the Mall and the Union Station train terminal. Three antique-appointed guest rooms and a library stocked with magazines and newspapers make for a comfortable night's stay. Breakfasts prepared with local produce and a gourmet's flair provide fuel for a day of sightseeing.

Georgetown Inn

$$ **96 rooms**
1310 Wisconsin Ave. NW, Georgetown. 202-333-8900 or 888-587-2388. www.georgetown inn.com.

Combining European elegance and colonial charm, the Georgetown Inn sits along bustling Wisconsin Avenue, in the heart of tony Georgetown's shops and restaurants. Luxurious marble bathrooms and heavenly four-poster beds lend an air of regal warmth to a hotel that has housed the Duke and Duchess of Windsor during past visits to Washington, DC.

Kalorama Guest House

$$ **30 rooms**
1854 Mintwood Pl. NW, Adams Morgan. 202-667-6369 or 800-974-6250. www.kaloramaguest house.com.

Nestled in culturally diverse Adams Morgan, this charming assortment of Victorian town houses pampers visitors with homey comforts, such as afternoon sherry and tasty continental breakfast selections. Rooms are sparse and simple, tinged with Victorian flair that mirrors the vibrant and well-loved neighborhood.

Hotel Lombardy

$$ **136 rooms**
2019 Pennsylvania Ave. NW, Foggy Bottom. 202-828-2600 or 800-424-5486. www.hotel lombardy.com.

Restored to reflect its original 1929 character, the Hotel Lombardy is located just four blocks from

the White House in the center of Washington's business district. Sumptuous bedding complements the densely woven oriental rugs and sleek chrome bath fixtures. Technological amenities coexist with the quaint ambience of this bastion of traditional DC hospitality. Hotel guests are entitled to passes to the outdoor pool at the nearby Washington Plaza Hotel.

Hotel Rouge

$$ **137 rooms**
1315 16th St. NW, Dupont Circle. 202-232-8000 or 800-738-1202. www.rougehotel.com.

Hotel Rouge

David Phelps/Destination DC

You can't help seeing red at this luxury boutique property on Embassy Row. True to its name, red is the color theme carried throughout the edgy décor of the lobby, the rooms and the sleek Bar Rouge. You'll even be welcomed with a complimentary Bloody Mary when you check in. If you feel like cooking, the hotel offers Chow Rooms, equipped with stainless-steel kitchenettes. Just want to kick back? Chill Rooms feature two 27-inch Sony flat-screen TVs and a Sony PlayStation that doubles as a DVD player. Hotel Rouge prides itself on pride—it's known as a gay-friendly establishment.

Hotel Tabard Inn

$$ 40 rooms
1739 N St. NW, Dupont Circle. 202-785-1277. www.tabardinn.com.

A Dupont Circle institution for more than 80 years, this hotel oozes charm with its scarlet walls, twisting staircases, stained-glass lamps and heavy antique furnishings. You have to walk up to your room here (there's no elevator). Eclectic guest quarters vary in size and décor; some share bathrooms. For lunch or dinner, you can savor acclaimed New American fare at the inn's heralded **restaurant ($$$)**, in its simple dining room or in the walled garden. A continental breakfast is included in the room tab. The live jazz often played in one of the hotel's Victorian sitting areas is also on the house.

Woodley Park Guest House

$$ 18 rooms
2647 Woodley Rd., NW, Woodley Park. 202-667-0218 or 866-667-0218. www.woodleyparkguest house.com.

A friendly staff and a big continental breakfast make stays at this B&B memorable. Clean, cozy, and comfortable, the Woodley Park blends warm hospitality with modern amenities. Fine antiques provide an atmosphere of sophistication, while such touches as wireless internet access make more modern statements.

BUDGET

Hereford House

$ 4 rooms
604 South Carolina Ave. SE, Capitol Hill. 202-543-0102.

English hospitality welcomes guests at this Capitol Hill B&B. Settle back in the parlor, have a proper cup of tea, and let owner Ann Edwards fill you in on what to see and do in the neighborhood—the Capitol and the Library of Congress are just a pleasant 10-minute walk away. Four individually decorated rooms—with no TVs or phones to bother you—share two baths. You'll start your day off with a hearty complimentary breakfast. Pets are allowed with permission, but this property doesn't cotton to kids under 12.

The Inn at Dupont Circle South

$ 8 rooms
1312 19th St. NW, Dupont Circle. 202-467-6777 or 866-467-2100. www.thedupontcollection.com.

Stepping into The Inn at Dupont Circle South is like walking into an old friend's home. Innkeeper Carolyn greets everyone by name and goes above and beyond the call of duty to make her guests happy and comfortable. It's no wonder many of her guests keep in touch after they return home. Carolyn makes omelettes every morning and the location across the street from the Metro is a major plus.

HOTELS BY THEME

Looking for the best business hotels in Washington or a posh place to take tea? Want to bring Fido along? In the preceding pages, we've organized the properties by price category, so below we've broken them out by theme to help you plan your trip.

Antique Charm
Hotel Tabard Inn (p153)
The Madison Hotel (p149)
Morrison-Clark Inn (p150)
Woodley Park Guest House (p153)

Budget Beaters
The Inn at Dupont Circle (p153)
Hereford House (p153)
Kalorama Guest House (p152)

For Business Travelers
Beacon Hotel (p148)
Hotel Lombardy (p152)
Jurys Washington (p149)
The Liaison Capitol Hill (p146)
Mandarin Oriental Hotel (p144)
One Washington Circle (p150)
Ritz-Carlton, Washington, DC (p145)

Hip Décor
Hotel George (p146)
Hotel Helix (p148)
Hotel Rouge (p152)
The Liaison Capitol Hill (p146)

Hotels for Tea
Four Seasons Hotel (p144)
Hay-Adams (p146)
Hereford House (p153)
Renaissance Mayflower
   Hotel (p147)
Ritz-Carlton, Washington, DC (p145)

Hotels with a View
Channel Inn Hotel (p151)
W Washington DC (p147)
St. Regis, Washington, DC (p145)
Washington Court Hotel (p147)
Watergate Hotel (p145)
Willard InterContinental (p148)

Hotels with History
Doolittle Guest House (p151)
Hay-Adams (p146)
Henley Park Hotel (p148)
Hotel Tabard Inn (p153)
The Mansion on O Street (p146)
Morrison-Clark Inn (p150)
Omni Shoreham (p150)
Renaissance Mayflower
   Hotel (p147)

Helix Suite, Helix Hotel

David Phelps/Kimpton Group

Hotels that Might Make Al Gore Smile

Several Washington hotels have proudly jumped on the green bandwagon. At Hotel Madera *(1310 New Hampshire Ave NW)* and the Topaz Hotel *(1733 N St NW)* hybrid cars park for free. The Embassy Suites *(4300 Military Rd)* now has energy-efficient heating and cooling systems in every suite and even prints with soy-based ink. And, both the Embassy Suites and the Marriott at Metro Center *(775 12th Street NW)* recently switched from chemically treated to saline-treated pools.

WASHINGTON, DC

The following abbreviations may appear in this Index: NHS National Historic Site; NM National Monument; NMem National Memorial; NP National Park; NHP National Historical Park; NRA National Recreational Area; NWR National Wildlife Refuge; SP State Park; SHP State Historical Park; SHS State Historic Site.

INDEX

INDEX

List of Maps

Photo Credits (page Icons)
Must Know
©Blackred/iStockphoto.com *Star Attractions:* 6-9
©Nigel Carse/iStockphoto.com *Calendar of Events:* 10-11
©Richard Cano/iStockphoto.com *Practical Information:* 12-19
Must Sees
©PhotoDisc *Government Sites:* 22-29, *Memorials:* 56-63, *Nearby Northern Virginia:* 106-117
©Terraxplorer/iStockphoto.com *Museums:* 30-55
©Marcos Carvalho/Bigstockphtoo.com *Historic Sites:* 64-73
©Helen Roach/Dreamstime.com *Neighborhoods:* 74-79
©Scott Cramer/iStockphoto.com *Parks and Gardens:* 80-81
©Kutt Niinepuu/Dreamstime.com *Excursions:* 118-129

Must Dos
©Yurovskikh Aleksander/iStockphoto.com *Fun:* 82-87
©Michael Walker/iStockphoto.com *Kids:* 88-92
©Shannon Workman/Bigstockphoto.com *Performing Arts:* 93-95
©Alex Slobodkin/iStockphoto.com *Shop:* 96-99
©Jill Chen/iStockphoto.com *Nightlife:* 100-103
©ImageDJ *Spas:* 104-105
©Marie-France Bélanger/iStockphoto.com *Restaurants:* 130-143
©Larry Roberg/iStockphoto.com *Hotels:* 144-155

INDEX